THE BICYCLE TEST

Finding Belief, Purpose, and Hope after a Traumatic Brain Injury

Damian Wąsowicz

CONTENTS

PART IV: My challenges and the road to recovery

PART V: My life since the accident

ACKNOWLEDGEMENTS

I would like to sincerely thank all of those mentioned and not mentioned in this book for your support during my recovery. Your presence, love, thoughts, and prayers have been instrumental in helping me get my life together again. In particular, thank you to the paramedics and medical staff at the Union and Milpark Hospitals. Thank you to all the individuals who helped me to write this book, especially Larry O'Sullivan, gone yet not forgotten, who helped me to put my words on paper and start writing *The Bicycle Test*.

This book is dedicated to all those who have experienced trauma of any kind. I hope that my story will help you in your unique recovery process.

PART I

THE ACCIDENT

1

HEAD-ON

Something big … and white … hit me while I was on my bicycle.

This is my last memory, and a very hazy one I have, even today, of the accident.

I somersaulted into the air, my body crashing into this speeding monstrosity of steel, my head going through its windshield and smacking into its steering wheel. My journey did not end there. My body was flung over the roof and into the back of the service vehicle, which was filled with rubbish … so at least I was afforded a soft landing.

I immediately lapsed into a state of unconsciousness.

My elder brother, Waldek, and my younger one, Adrian, screamed my name, panic and urgency in their voices. They jumped off their bicycles and rushed down the hill to find me. My bicycle was a mangled mess on one side of the road, with the pickup truck, which had eventually come to a stop, off the road to the other side. My brothers had heard the crunch and deafening sound of the impact, but they hadn't seen me land. They were frantic in their search for me.

I lay there, on the back of the bakkie, in a bed of junk, bleeding, and choking on my own blood.

The driver was in a state of shock, fearing he had killed me. He was arguing with Waldek, refusing to drive for help.

There was no cell phone reception in the area where we had been cycling, Suikerbosrand Nature Reserve, a climbing mecca for cyclists that is approximately an hour's drive from Johannesburg and near the town of Heidelberg. It is known as one of the most idyllic game reserves in the region and has abundant flora and fauna, making it a popular spot for hiking, cycling, and picnicking.

I was critical and needed help fast. Adrian, who was still a scholar and 16 years of age, sat with me in my landing place. I was rasping for breath, so he held my mouth open so that I could breathe, and with his other hand held my degloved face together. I later learnt that the word "degloved" is used to describe a severe injury where an extensive section of skin is completely torn off the underlying tissue. I was in a mess.

Waldek took matters into his own hands. He removed the glass from the driver's seat, the remnants of the windshield that shattered as my head went hurtling through it to connect with the steering wheel. He also had to kick out a part of the windshield that was dangling precariously over the steering wheel so that he had clear visibility to drive. He then jumped behind the wheel, leaving the driver to stand in the road and mutter to himself.

Waldek needed to find help for me, and he needed to find it very fast! He knew the reserve pretty well, as we had cycled there on many occasions. He recalled there was a Protea Hotel not too far from us, about eight kilometres away, and he deemed this our best bet in this isolated part of the world. They would have cell phone reception to get medical help, and surely they would have a first-aid kit and someone proficient at first aid, or, even better, a doctor staying at the hotel.

Waldek brought the service vehicle to a screeching halt at the entrance to the hotel and ran into the reception screaming for help and a doctor. Adrian remained in the back of the vehicle with my unconscious body, covered with my blood. The poor kid, he was in shock, watching the colour, life, and blood drain from his comatose brother in his arms.

Help was slow in arriving. None of the hotel staff members knew anything about first aid, where the first-aid kit was stored, or what the emergency contact numbers were.

I'm not sure if it was luck, destiny, or part of God's plan that when Waldek was imploring someone to come and help me, a certain gentleman passed through the reception area and noticed what was happening.

Mr Nigel Henderson, a South African who was unknown to us, had just married an Irish woman and was on honeymoon, visiting Suikerbosrand Nature Reserve. He just happened to be at the Protea Hotel at that very moment. Nigel had obtained basic medical training through his service in the South African and British armies and was able to play a role in giving me as much crude medical attention as he could offer in the circumstances, and to stabilise me while waiting for the emergency services to arrive. Nigel's wife insisted that they cover and keep me in blankets in the meantime, as at that stage I was going into shock.

It still took several hours for me to receive the correct medical attention. The hotel staff finally phoned the local emergency numbers for help, and it took about 30 minutes for the paramedics to arrive. Then, recognising the seriousness of my condition, they deemed it necessary for me to be airlifted to hospital. It took another 45 minutes for the chopper to eventually come.

By this time, Waldek and Adrian were in shock. The weather had turned, and it became cold. Both were still in their cycling clothes, covered with my blood. My brothers had acted purely on adrenalin, rushing to get me help, arguing with the hotel staff, enduring frustration at the slowness of the medical help and, in all honesty, not realising the gravity of my condition. Other than the blood haemorrhaging that resulted from the degloving of my face, and the blood in my mouth, there were no outward signs, physically, to indicate how broken my body really was.

According to the paramedics, I registered a 7/15 at the scene of the accident on the Glasgow Coma Scale (GCS). The GCS is a 15-point scale for estimating and categorising the severity of brain injury. The test measures an injured person's motor and verbal responses, as well as their ability to open their eyes. My score fell into the severe disability range, which implies coma and an unconscious state – no meaningful response and no voluntary movements.

I was intubated, immobilised, and airlifted to Union Hospital, a private, Netcare hospital in Alberton, about 40 kilometres away.

By this time, I had lost four of the six litres of blood in my body.

What was meant to be a peaceful Monday morning cycle in a secure nature reserve turned into me lapsing into a state of unconsciousness, fighting for my life, fighting for survival.

2

WHAT HAPPENED WHILE I WAS UNCONSCIOUS?

While I was being taken to hospital, a ranger from Suikerbosrand helped Waldek and Adrian to fetch their bicycles, my mangled helmet and bike, and then to drive them to the hospital.

Earlier, while Nigel and the paramedics were attending to me, Waldek called his wife, Pauline, and my girlfriend, Alexandra, and told them that I'd come off my bicycle, was unconscious, and was being treated by the medical personnel. Later, Waldek updated the message to say that I was being airlifted to Union Hospital and that they could meet him and Adrian there.

My parents, who live in Vanderbijlpark, some 70 kilometres south of Johannesburg, were spending a few days with Waldek and his family, as Pauline had recently given birth to their second grandchild. They were not that far from the hospital and arrived just in time to see the helicopter arriving and me being rushed into the casualty ward.

Upon admission, I was hypotensive, meaning I had abnormally low blood pressure, and I had to be resuscitated. My GCS had dropped to 2T/10T. Given that I was intubated, the verbal component fell away and the GCS was measured on a 10-point scale; 2T implied the lowest-possible score – no opening of the eyes, and no motor response.

Secondary metabolic complications occurred as a result of hypovolaemic shock, which is a life-threatening condition caused by losing too much blood; hypoxia, where plasma and oxygen concentration in the blood drops to dangerously low levels; hypercarbia, in which carbon dioxide levels in the blood are elevated to abnormally high levels; and acidosis, which involves having elevated levels of acid in the blood and other body tissues. I was anaemic.

By the time my brothers arrived at the casualty ward, I was already hooked up to a breathing machine and monitors, and concerned but well-trained personnel attended to me. My temperature was very low, so they used hot-water bottles to help stabilise my condition.

Doctors questioned my family to learn more about my health, allergies, blood group, and medical-aid details.

After a while, the leading doctor approached the family and said, "Your son is critical. I suggest you pray for him and that you also pray for me."

This was a massive blow to my family and girlfriend, for they had not fully realised the seriousness of my condition.

Being Catholic, calls were made to our family and friends, asking them all to pray for my life and recovery. It was also posted on Facebook, and these calls and messages reached people in Poland, Israel, and in various parts of South Africa. My friends and colleagues at work were contacted and informed of the dire situation I was in.

A Polish priest from our church, Father Fausten Jankowski, who looked after the Polish community in both Johannesburg and Vanderbijlpark, visited my bedside and prayed for me. He gave me the Last Rites, a sacrament through which Catholics receive last prayers and ministrations, when possible, shortly before death. At the same time, Father Jankowski comforted my parents, brothers, and close acquaintances who had arrived. This was indeed a wonderful gesture of love and support.

I had a blood transfusion, my face was stapled together, glass was removed from my body, and due to the trauma my body was subjected to, I was induced into a comatose state. I also underwent a series of X-rays and associated tests to determine the extent of the damage. I was given a less-than 5% chance of survival.

Later that evening, when my family was allowed to see me for the first time, they received an even bigger shock. My physical condition had deteriorated significantly since being airlifted to hospital. My head was almost twice its normal size, my ears were virtually invisible, and my eyes had sunk deep into the swelling. The staples around my face made my appearance look even more dehumanising. My family was later told that the way I looked was a blessing in disguise, as the numerous cracks in my skull had allowed my brain to swell without the increasing pressure, which would have resulted in even more severe traumatic brain injury (TBI). The doctors did a tracheostomy on my neck, whereby they made a cut in the windpipe to help my breathing, and they also did a gastrostomy, which involves making an opening into the stomach that can be used to feed a patient. I also had an array of pipes, monitors, and machines hooked up to my broken body. Not a pretty sight.

I survived the night.

The next day, a number of doctors and specialists held a meeting to decide what types of treatments to give me, and which ones to prioritise, in order to stabilise my condition; that is, if I survived at all.

Over the next couple of days, I had a series of operations. Firstly, the doctors needed to clear my sinus passage, which was full of shattered frontal bone, which is the bone in the forehead part of the skull and the upper part of the eye sockets. My nose, jaw, cheeks, and eye sockets were broken and had to be reset.

Titanium plates were inserted into my face to correct this. My teeth had to be repositioned in their original places and were held by wires. All four lobes of the skull were fractured, leading to severe brain injury. I suffered a spinal injury consisting of numerous compressed discs and eight fractured vertebrae. The impact of the accident on my chest led to fractured ribs and a lung contusion, which happens when the blood capillaries in a region of injured tissue have been ruptured. In addition, I suffered abdominal injury leading to laceration of the upper pole of the right kidney.

My shoulder was another major area for concern. The initial prognosis was that my arm had to be amputated and I was to be given an artificial limb. The hospital's leading specialist in this field was away in the USA for a conference, so, thank God, Waldek forced a decision to leave my shoulder until this person's return to South Africa a couple of days later. This turned out to be the right decision.

I still had problems in other areas of my body that needed corrective surgery, but I was deemed too weak to withstand another operation, and it would be a risk to do anything until I stabilised.

PART II

MY LIFE BEFORE
THE ACCIDENT

3

COMMUNIST
POLAND

I was born on 22 January 1980, and lived with Waldek and my
mother and father, Danuta and Franciszek, in a small village,
Wojkowice Kościelne. Our village was in the administrative
district of Gmina Siewierz, within Będzin County, Silesian
Voivodeship, in southern Poland. It lay approximately 11
kilometres south-west of Siewierz, 14 kilometres north-east of
Będzin, and 24 kilometres north-east of the regional capital,
Katowice.

It was not easy growing up in a communistic environment.
Things were tough, but Waldek and I never went to bed without
a meal. We enjoyed the love and closeness of our family and
received the best-possible education available to us in our village.
Birthdays and Christmases were a real treat for Waldek and me,
as we also received gifts from our grandparents and extended
family. Although we may not have felt as privileged as some in
the world, we were so much better off than many others on this
planet and many in Poland, for which we are eternally grateful.

Although I was too young to understand it all, Poland went through some massive changes, both from a political and an economic point of view. Some of the influences that formed the background to my upbringing in Poland were the strikes of the early 1980s, the birth and subsequent banning of the Solidarity movement, economic sanctions by some Western countries, privatisation of the state's assets, changes in the social mood of the people, and the involvement of the Catholic Church in the affairs of Poland.

It was important for the people of the country to show their Catholicism, especially in a communist state. The Communist Party representatives had contacted my mom on several occasions and tried to coerce her to join their party, which implied giving up one's beliefs and becoming an atheist; they even went as far as threatening that they would have her fired from her job should she not comply.

My mom held out resolutely and was not swayed by the pressure they brought to bear on her. She had witnessed how her father, my beloved grandfather, was forced to join the Communist Party. My grandfather had five children. My mom was the third child and one of four daughters. My mom loved farming and wanted to go to university to complete her Agricultural Sciences degree. She was not permitted to study at university until my grandfather joined the Communist Party, as students whose families belonged to the party received extra credits and bonus marks because of that affiliation.

Being brought up in Poland, which is more than 90% Roman Catholic, my brother Waldek and I attended Holy Mass at least three times a week and became altar boys, a very important function and status within the church. I made my first confession and then later partook in my first Holy Communion. The latter was a big event, especially in Communist Poland, and the community packed out the church for it.

We had witnessed religious statues and crosses being removed from schools and government places. Fortunately, this did not extend to confiscating one's religious icons or intruding into one's home on a religious quest.

Waldek had already made his first confession and partaken in Holy Communion.

Easter and Christmas were also massive events, not only for the Church, but within our community. For Christmas, usually the priest would go and pray with the members of the community in their own homes, at the same time imploring God's blessing and protection over the home and its inhabitants.

Sometimes, the priest would linger and enjoy a hot cup of coffee and something warm to eat before moving on to the next house and repeating the process. He would always ask the altar boys to accompany him on these visits. So, there we were, trudging from house to house in the bitterly cold conditions and through the piled-up snow. At times, we were forced, or should I say encouraged, to sing carols or other religious hymns. I really did not enjoy this part; I cannot sing. But, it had its advantages: the people would give us sweets and we also had a chance to see all the pretty girls in the village, have warm meals, and even sneak a sip of the wine reserved for the church service.

Despite the effects of communism on our lives, Waldek and I had a wonderful childhood, much better than many other children in Poland did. We were considered above middle class.

One thing for sure is that if I had remained in Poland, I would never have been hit off my bicycle by a service vehicle in Suikerbosrand. But who knows what fate has in store for us? How many times we come to forks in the road and life takes us on a particular route.

4

FOOD RATIONING AND SCARCITY

Back in the 1980s, foodstuffs and luxuries were extremely scarce. This even extended to medical equipment. The shop, which was the only one in the village, belonged to the state. The shelves were often bare, and due to the economic conditions prevalent in Poland, certain foods and luxuries were not imported into the country.

But Waldek and I found an ingenious way to sample some of these goodies.

We lived on the top floor of a double-storey building we shared with two other families – an old couple who lived downstairs, and my friend's family, who lived next door to us. We rented this accommodation from the government. A few hundred metres from our house was an overnight stop for the large trucks that travelled through Poland and which went past our house on the main road out of town. In many cases, these trucks were travelling either to or from neighbouring countries, and they carried goods from Western European states.

Waldek and I would mingle with and talk to the drivers, and invariably they would be eating or drinking some product they brought with them. This is how we were introduced to luxuries such as viennas. It is quite ironic that we deemed viennas, a highly processed food, to be luxuries just because we could not easily obtain them. They tasted like cardboard in comparison to the traditional Polish sausages called *kiełbasa*.

Food and other items were rationed and bought with stamps. Often, we had to queue for a long time to buy something. Once, I was ill, and my dad had to drive from village to village to find an antibiotic and some cough mixture for me.

5

FISHING
FOR SUCKERS

Coffee was a luxury item that we could only get one packet of per month. Often, our mom would ask Waldek or me to queue for her at the shop; she would join us much later to buy the coffee.

One day, I went with my mother to get a packet. The queue was long … it felt like we had waited two hours just to get in the front door. I estimated it would take us another 30 minutes or so to get to buy the coffee. Our village had a very small population of possibly only about 1 000 people, and it seemed as if half of them had turned out to buy their allotment of coffee that day.

The setup and the feel of the shop was very different to that of stores in other parts of the world. There was no counter, and there were no elaborate shop fittings. It was very basic and crude – just a table for a counter, and a woman, the shopkeeper, standing on the other side of it, serving her customers.

Sadly, on that day, the crowd became impatient and someone actually pushed the table a bit too much. This ruffled the shopkeeper's feathers. She said she was going to call the police, so we all just had to get out of her shop. We didn't get any coffee that day or for that month.

When the paper coffee packets were empty, my mother would save them on the top shelf in the kitchen, believing they would come in handy to store things in. My parents had grown up just after the Second World War and understood the value of not wasting anything, and of saving things for later use. They lived by the proverb, "waste not, want not".

One day, when my cousin was visiting us, we concocted the idea to see how many motorists we could trick into stopping their cars and getting out to fetch what they thought was a freebie packet of coffee just lying in the road, but which was in fact just a packet filled with sand.

We filled one packet, tied some fishing line to the end of it, and proceeded to the main road, behind a factory, to carry out our prank. Ironically, this was the same road on which a close friend of mine died.

We hid in the bushes beside the road. When a car would stop, we would pull the coffee packet, attached to the fishing line, further away from the person who got out to get what they thought was a bonus. It was great fun.

After successfully fooling a number of people, we looked up to see a car, similar to the one my parents had, coming to a stop in front of the coffee packet.

"Hey shit," Waldek shouted, "that is our parents' car."

We panicked and ran further into the field of tall grass and lay down so we could not be seen.

We saw my dad getting out the car to pick up the coffee packet. He noticed it was filled with sand, and he saw that it was attached to a fishing line trailing off the road. We were close enough to see the expression on his face; this work had the hallmark of his beloved-but-mischievous sons. We were also within earshot of his muttering to himself, "If I get to the house and those kids are not there, I will give them a double thrashing!"

Waldek, my cousin and I made a mad dash for home … but obviously we were too late. My dad saw us charging around the factory, trying to get home before him. He could see the guilt written all over our faces.

That was the last time the three of us played the coffee game. My dad gave each of us a hiding. I got hammered the worst because for some reason I was always seen as the naughty kid, the instigator, the troublemaker. Looking back, I believe they were probably correct.

6

SOŁTYS

My grandfather on my mother's side, Zenon Muraszewski, was one of those individuals who survived the horrors of war and the German camps. He was born on 4 July 1919 in a village called Grójczyk. In 1927, when he was eight years old, his parents bought a smallholding in Siemnówek village.

After completing five years of elementary schooling, and at the age of 14, he started working on a farm owned by a Jewish couple. In 1938, he became a member of the Polish Socialist Party, however his membership didn't last too long, as his parents convinced him to exit the party after a senior member of an opposing party started to spread false rumours of communists living in Siemnówek. Zenon left Siemnówek and found work on another farm, where he was treated fairly and rewarded justly for his work.

Around the time just before the Second World War broke out, the Poles feared that Germans living in Poland would sabotage infrastructure such as telephone lines, which were crucial for communications not only for the public but also for the military.

One evening, Zenon and his friends were on patrol to safeguard the telephone lines and the train tracks when they noticed a suspicious figure near the lines. They approached silently, but the person noticed them and tried to escape. They ran like horses for a couple hundred metres until they finally caught the would-be saboteur. Luckily, they managed to save the lines in time, and they handed the person over to the Polish military.

After the start of the Second World War, Zenon returned to the farm where he had previously worked in Siemnówek to find that the former Jewish owners had been deported and executed, with Germans now owning the farm.

In 1941, Zenon was taken to Łódź, where he was placed in a camp run by the SS Race and Settlement Office. Here he was evaluated by Schutzstaffel (SS) specialists, who found him fit to be included in the German race. To avoid the eventualities associated with Germanisation, he poured hydrated building lime into his eyes for a few weeks until eventually the alkaline burns caused permanent damage. By doing so, he saved himself from becoming the man the Germans wanted him to become, and a year after that, he was released.

He returned to his family's farm in Siemnówek. However, he didn't have peace for long, as in 1944, the whole family was taken away to Germany to do forced labour. He worked in that country until 1945, and after the war ended, he returned to Siemnówek. In 1946, he was granted a seven-hectare farm and he married Irena Bałszewska, with whom he had one son and four daughters.

In 1952, he was elected as Mayor ('*Sołtys*' in Polish) of Siemnówek, a position he held for 51 years until 2003. As the length of his tenure implies, he was a very popular person who was loved and supported by the community. With their support, he managed to secure substantial financial assistance for the village, which after years of war needed to be rebuilt.

A school, accommodation for teachers, and a fire station were built under his mayorship. He was also instrumental in ensuring that a much-needed shop was opened in the village which eliminated the need for the community to have to travel to a nearby town for their groceries. He also secured funding to turn an old, run-down farm track into a modern tar road. This might not sound like a big deal to us today, but at the time, and to the people of Siemnówek, this was a blessing, as it linked the small village to two towns, Lubraniec and Włocławek, via public transport. He also oversaw the installation of more telephone lines and street lights.

My grandfather's creed was, "Never approach the horse from the rear, as you may feel its hoofs. Never approach a bull from the front, as you may feel its horns. When approaching a politician, do so neither from the front nor from the rear; best to pass them from the side and from a far-off distance."

Although he was succeeded as mayor by a younger, capable man, until his dying day people would come to his house to seek his counsel, and he remained known to all as Sołtys.

I was blessed to have a grandfather like that, a person I could look up to, someone I really admired and someone who proved to be a great source of inspiration to me during my trying times.

Waldek and I spent most of our summer holidays with our grandparents on their farm, some 300 kilometres from our village. My parents had demanding, full-time jobs, and they were limited in terms of the number and timing of their annual leave days. So, it was arranged that we spend our holidays with our grandparents and our cousins, who would regularly join us at my grandparents' home.

We didn't just loaf about on the farm. Our grandfather gave all of us chores to do, and we helped with the harvesting, and with the feeding of the sheep, pigs, cows, and horses. By age eight or nine, I was already driving the tractor on the farm field during the harvest. It was not any big deal; all I had to do was keep the tractor in a straight line and when I got to one end of the farm, someone was waiting to swap places with me and turn the tractor around and into position for me to head back in the opposite direction, hopefully still in a straight line. On one occasion, I could not reach the brakes of the tractor and went hurtling off course, with my grandfather frantically chasing after me to stop the tractor.

My grandparents loved having us on the farm and took great care of us. They taught us so much and always supported and encouraged us. We had a lot of fun there, and often my grandfather would cover for Waldek and me when we caused trouble or needed to hide things from my parents. I recall one such instance when we made a *kettie*, a small, hand-held catapult used to shoot small stones. My mom hated the idea of us playing with such a dangerous toy.

Spending time with my grandparents and family was something very special to me, and even today, I recall fond memories of a happy and loved childhood.

My grandfather was well into his 90s when I had the accident, and despite the hardships he suffered during his life, he continued to live as a positive and upbeat man.

7

NAUGHTY KIDS

As kids, Waldek and I were regarded as mischievous. But when it came to discipline, we respected and listened to our elders; not only to our parents, but also to our grandparents, aunts and uncles, teachers, and the priest.

I would get into fights with other boys in my school, even those who were a little older or bigger than me. I was not afraid. I was a damn good fighter with a proud record of victories. But these scraps didn't come without a bloody nose, bruised knuckles, or a kick in the groin.

If some boy, a school grade higher or a year older than me, picked on Waldek, he would call me to come and fight that person. It wasn't that Waldek was afraid of the boy or was a weak fighter. In fact, he was very strong, confident, and an excellent fighter. I guess he did this to humiliate the opponent. If, however, the boy picking the fight with Waldek was older or in a higher school grade than Waldek, then Waldek took matters into his own hands and thumped the daylights out of him.

We used to play quite a lot in and around the stream near our home and which fed into the river further down at the end of the village. We had a lot of fun and enjoyed swimming and fishing in that stream. We didn't have fishing rods, as they weren't available at the shops in our village, so we used whatever we could think of. Initially, we would use bait and a tin, which we made a hole in, but this did not prove too profitable. We then progressed to use a net, but it wasn't a proper fishing one; we just made it work with whatever materials we had. The results, using this method, improved slightly.

At some stage, our fishing exploits evolved to the more-typical method of using a hook and some fishing line. We made our own fishing rods with branches from the trees near the stream.

Nevertheless, we still weren't too successful, so one day we came up with a creative plan. There was a small bridge constructed to allow people or a single car to cross over the stream to get to their homes, the shop, church, and other places. Waldek and I blocked the stream by putting a sheet of metal, which we'd gotten from home, into it, causing the water to dam up. The fish now circled in a very small area, which made it much easier to catch them.

Of course, we could only fish during the summer months, as in winter the weather would be bitterly cold and the stream would sometimes freeze over.

Once we'd caught what we deemed sufficient for our needs to take home for our mom to cook, we removed the metal sheet, allowing the water to again flow down to the river as we went on our merry way.

To our surprise, our mother was not impressed with our efforts, as the fish we caught were too small to be eaten. In fact, they were baby fish, so in the end we got into trouble for our efforts.

One of the other games we played along the banks of the stream was stone-skipping. We would throw a stone or pebble across the surface of the water, hoping it would bounce a number of times and skim to the other bank. We started to improve with practice and managed to get our stones to bounce three or four times. As the stream was very narrow, we used to angle our stone-skipping competition mainly along the length of the water rather than the width of the stream.

We also started to appreciate that there was a technique to getting the stone or pebble to skip across the water without sinking. The key was the speed with which you propelled the object. We realised the harder or quicker we tossed it, the better were our chances of achieving the maximum number of bounces. We also realised that the angle at which one casts the stone is vital. The larger the stone, the more acute the angle should be.

For some reason, on this particular day, Waldek, his friends and I got separated and we ended up opposite each other, with Waldek on the other side of the stream. As per Murphy's Law, I aimed a bit skew and as I let go of a fairly large stone, I saw it bouncing off the water and heading directly towards Waldek. Before I could even shout a warning, the stone shot off the water's surface and hit Waldek on the side of the forehead, just above the eye, immediately drawing blood.

We jumped on our bicycles and made a mad dash for home, rushing past our mother towards the bathroom.

My mom called out, "*Waldek, Damian czy wszystko jest w porządku?* (Waldek, Damian, is everything okay?)"

"*Tak Mamuś, wszystko ok!* (Yes, Mommy, it's okay!)" was our reply. My main mission was to obscure Waldek from my mom so that she didn't notice his bloody face, and to find something in the bathroom to stop the bleeding.

A little while later, our mom suddenly appeared at the bathroom door and saw me trying to wash my brother's face and stop the bleeding. There was blood everywhere, on our clothes, all over the basin, and on the floor. It really looked worse than it was. Fortunately, Waldek didn't need stitches, but he bore the marks on his forehead for quite some time.

It was a crude reminder to me of how quickly accidents can happen, even when one is just playing games or having fun. I did experience many bumps along the way, some not too bad or painful, but others, especially those that happened while playing soccer or hockey or riding my bicycle, were tests to see what the body could withstand. But nothing ... nothing at all could have prepared me for that life-changing crash that put me into a coma for 14 days.

Incidentally, the current world record for stone-skipping, as per the *Guinness Book of World Records*, is 88 bounces, achieved by Kurt Steiner in 2013 ... If only Kurt achieved this fabulous record when I was still a kid in Poland, I'm sure he would have been my hero!

8

IMMIGRATION TO SOUTH AFRICA – A CULTURE SHOCK

The move from Poland to South Africa, back in August 1990, was a momentous change for all of us, particularly from an emotional and cultural point of view. We came from a little village in Poland and ended up in the rather large town of Vanderbijlpark.

My dad, Frank, had been granted a three-year contract to work for Iscor, in the steel industry. I was only 10 years old at that stage; Waldek was 11. Funny enough, it had been my dad's dream to live or work in South Africa since his school days. Sadly, due to the political situation in Poland, there were great restrictions on people leaving the country. I understand from my mother that they didn't want the outside world to know what was happening in Poland. If the authorities got wind of people wanting to leave the country, they would simply confiscate their passports. There was a small opportunity back in 1980 when a few of my dad's friends were granted jobs in South Africa. I was only six months old and Waldek was 15 months of age. My mom stopped that plan dead in its tracks. She rightly could not travel and start all over in a strange country with two young children.

We arrived in South Africa with four suitcases that weighed not more than 12 kilograms each (the maximum allowance granted to travellers), an English dictionary, some money, jewellery, and our computer. That was all. We left Poland in the middle of the night when friends drove us to Austria. Someone was to arrange temporary accommodation for us in that country, but he let us down. So we slept on the floor in the basement of a building for two days until we could catch our connecting flight to South Africa.

We couldn't tell anyone we were leaving for fear of having our passports confiscated.

Iscor hosted us for two months at the Shakespeare Inn, full board. It was fun, and Waldek and I really enjoyed the swimming pool. Coming from Poland, we didn't find the water to be cold. We wondered why we were the only two kids in the pool, and everyone, wearing jerseys, thought we were mad.

It wasn't long after our arrival in South Africa that we had to start looking for our own accommodation. We found a two-bedroom house to rent. For furniture we managed to purchase four plastic chairs, a table, and four mattresses, from the OK Bazaars. There were no bases for the mattresses, so we literally slept on the floor.

My mom tried to get a job. With all her experience and degrees in agriculture we thought it would be a good fit for a business in South Africa. Unfortunately, most of the agricultural entities were run by Afrikaans-speaking people, and this did not work out. We had to rely solely on my dad's income.

My parents opened an account with the local store, and we could buy a few essentials on credit. This included a fridge, and a tiny black-and-white TV. After walking everywhere for several months, my parents decided enough was enough and they purchased a car on an instalment plan.

At that time, South Africa, not unlike Poland, was in the grip of political change. On arrival, we were greeted with a great deal of political uncertainty, violence, and unrest. The security forces were on high alert. Fortunately, with Nelson Mandela's release from prison, the way was paved for a democratic and peaceful solution.

Then there was the shock of learning a new language. From Polish to English and Afrikaans. Vanderbijlpark was predominantly Afrikaans-speaking.

School was another challenge. Waldek and I were enrolled at the local school. I was placed in Grade 2; Waldek in Grade 3. Initially, we didn't have school shoes or the school's uniform, so we attended in our civvies and tackies. Our parents managed to put some money together relatively quickly to suit us up in the school's uniform. However, owing to the fact that the school shoes were made of leather, they were quite expensive … and given this, we had to forgo shoes for quite some time.

One day, the teacher wrote a message to the class on the blackboard: "PLEASE REMEMBER TO POLISH YOUR SHOES BEFORE COMING TO SCHOOL TOMORROW".

When I read this, I literally became the incarnation of so many Eastern European jokes which we all, including me, laugh at these days. With my limited understanding of English, I believed that the message was aimed at Waldek and me to ensure that we would arrive at school with proper shoes the next day. We went home to our parents, with tears in our eyes that afternoon, and informed them of the message. They seemed concerned, but owing to the lack of money, the status quo remained. It was only later that I learnt that to "polish" one's shoes is spelt the same as "Polish", referring to people of Polish descent.

At least food, clothing, and medicine was not as scarce as it was in Poland. Cars were easily accessible and available in South Africa. Back in those days in Poland, for you to have a car you had to be very well-off, not so much from a financial point of view but with regard to your status. Your name had to go on a government list, and then you had to wait for your turn to get government permission to purchase the vehicle. Members of the Communist Party and those in mining were given preference. In South Africa, if you ordered a car, you only had to wait a month or two before you could buy it. In Poland, you could wait up to several years. My dad had to make pre-payments to secure his car in Poland. It took him six years to do this. Only when the car was fully paid for, in advance, could he take delivery of the vehicle.

Unlike in South Africa, in Poland cars were sold without a motor plan; that term and concept simply did not exist. I recall the tedious task of changing the car's brake pads and bleeding the brakes from time to time. Our dad would always call upon us to assist in the task. Changing the brake pads was a breeze. Every so often, Frank's strong arm would emerge from beneath his yellow Fiat 126 as he requested a particular spanner size. Waldek would always mess this up, and it would be my time to shine by always providing my dad with the correct spanner. At that brief moment, I would be seen, at least only by my dad, as the smarter kid … if only for a while.

Bleeding brakes was a totally different game. It required Waldek and I to press the brake pedal in and out continuously. This felt like a century of burning pain in our thighs before our dad would scream out "STOP!" and we could change positions. However, after a short break, we would be at it again, experiencing another century of continuous pain! Although it sometimes came at the expense of being involved, I loved my dad's ability to be so extremely handy, be that working on a car in Poland or in South Africa or anything one can possibly imagine.

What really shocked me the most was that in the South African suburbs, where we too were now living, there was virtually nothing going on; there weren't many people on the streets. People stayed indoors or in their offices. Perhaps it had to do with the crime and political agitation within the country.

Also, a very noticeable difference was the fact that South Africa had cell phones and phones. In Poland, it was totally different because, back in our village in the 1980s, we didn't have cell phones or phones in our homes. So, if you wanted to talk to or play with anyone or even mingle with people, you had to be out in the streets.

If you were to take an aerial shot of the streets of towns in Poland, you would see people there, whereas in South Africa it was completely different. Here, one seldom walked into a home on an unannounced visit. In general, a person first phoned the other party or made prior arrangements to visit; they didn't just pitch up. In some cases, if they did arrive unannounced, they might find that their host was put out or even visibly upset.

I do not understand. I have been in this country for 30 years, and even today this pattern remains. Why can't people – someone you know, a friend, or a neighbour – just walk up to your front door and visit you?

One reason I have discovered in later years is that some people like to ensure their house is clean to welcome visitors; others like to make sure they have something to offer you to eat or drink – and if they don't, they might feel embarrassed. I still find these reasons to be absurd.

9

MY LOVE
FOR CYCLING

I enjoy a very close bond with my brothers and parents. I believe this closeness emanates from the fact that when we, as an immigrant family, arrived in South Africa in 1990, we had no other family or close friends. Adrian blessed our lives some many years later.

Us three siblings shared some common interests, including soccer, cycling, and a great social life. Adrian was a bit young, but Waldek and I were party animals and enjoyed our fellowship with our mates, drinking beer and having lots of fun.

Waldek and I always enjoyed cycling. I recall drawing pictures in Poland of bicycles I aspired to ride when I was a bit older; these were no works of art, but in my mind the bikes they portrayed were machines that could take me all around the country and even beyond the Iron Curtain.

Waldek and I cycled almost daily with our friends. Perhaps it's in the genes: our dad loved to ride his Bianchi bicycle in his youth. Funny enough, many years later, Waldek and I became proud owners of our own Bianchi bikes ... in my mind, they are like those machines from the artistic drawings of my youth.

The whole of Poland was captured by the national cycle race called the Peace Tour, which was last held in 2006 and comprised a number of stage races through the countryside of Poland. This was the largest sporting event in Poland, and in its later years consisted of seven or eight stages totalling approximately 1 200 kilometres. The race was held annually and passed through more than 400 cities and towns in Poland and in what was in those times called East Germany and Czechoslovakia. Along its route, over two million spectators came to cheer and encourage the cyclists.

Waldek and I thought it a great idea to put together our own version of the Peace Tour. So, together with a group of our friends, we mapped out our own route around and out of the village.

The course wasn't an easy one for kids our age, but it was something that allowed us not only to test our cycling skills but also to challenge the limits of our imagination by pushing against all that we knew at that time: our physical limits, the limits of our neighbourhoods, and the limits of what our parents would allow.

The most dangerous part of the route was the section where we had to cycle on the apex of the local dam wall. If any of us took a tumble, God only knows what would've happened to that child. And, if my mom or dad caught us traversing the dam wall like that, heaven knows the extent of the trouble we would have been in. It's amazing how fearless one is as a child. It's also a fact of life that most of us become more fearful the older or more mature we get.

When we arrived at a nearby town, we all enjoyed a delicious and well-deserved ice-cream, then we cycled back home. In total, our own Peace Tour was only about ten kilometres long, but for us youngsters, it was as tough and gruelling and equally harsh as the formal Peace Tour route. It was a test we set for ourselves that provided a great sense of accomplishment when we passed it.

Cycling gave us a sense of freedom. It took us closer to the wonder of nature, the incredible sights and beauty of the scenery around us.

Later, in South Africa, I realised that we often take the magnificence of our surroundings for granted. When one of my cousins from Poland was visiting South Africa, we took her to see some of the wildlife and the sights, and she remarked that we were living in one of the most beautiful countries in the world. Yet, so many people in this country fail to see its beauty, for some or other reason.

I too had, at first, failed to see the allure of South Africa as I isolated myself between four walls: those of my home, my garage, my car, and of my office. How many other people are, like I was, trapped within the confines of their lives? For example, those who are in a loveless or an abusive marriage; those who are stuck in a job they hate; or those who sit alone in an apartment? And what about those who are addicted to nicotine, drugs, or alcohol, and who are searching for freedom, hope, or the light at the end of the tunnel?

Cycling enabled me to escape those four walls, to get the necessary exercise for my body, and to see this beautiful world. It also, by the strain on the body, made me realise the heights of mountains and depths of valleys and the contrasts in the weather conditions; from snow to blazing heat, from gale-force winds to utter calmness.

My bicycle rides took me on routes one wouldn't usually travel by car in South Africa, especially those that went into or through cities. I recall once cycling in what was termed a "dodgy" area in South Africa, one where unemployment and substance abuse were said to be rife. However, on passing through, we encountered no problems. The street was clean; there was no litter lying around. In fact, hardly any cars passed along the roads, meaning there were no potholes or oil spills that made matters hazardous for cyclists.

During this trip, I noticed a couple leaving their home, dressed like they were going to the opera. The man was in his tuxedo, and his companion was in her Sunday best, as they walked hand in hand to the nearby church service. If I hadn't been cycling through this area, I would never have experienced such a sight.

The great thing about cycling with Waldek and my friends was the companionship and the chance to give our bodies exercise in an enjoyable manner, which also helped to get our figures back into shape after all our partying and beer-drinking sessions. At least, that was our logic. What happened in reality was that after a good cycling session, which could be anything up to 150 kilometres or four or five hours long, we would then find a watering hole where we could relax, re-energise, and enjoy each other's company while relishing a coffee, some breakfast, and occasionally downing a few cold ones.

10

MY STUDENT AND WORKING DAYS

Our move to South Africa was a costly affair. Not only did we have to leave behind a house full of furniture and contents, meaning we had to start afresh, but we also had to rely on only one income stream: my dad's. The languages, English and Afrikaans, were stumbling blocks for all of us, but we had to learn, *fast*. Waldek and I picked the languages up much quicker than my poor mom did; she spoke Polish, German, and Russian. My mom ended up going for English lessons, whereas my dad picked up English and Afrikaans through his work.

My mom started a garden-service business and then moved on to take a post at an estate agency, selling houses. Often, Waldek or I had to help out by answering the phone and translating for my mom.

I did very well academically at school and loved sports. I was very good at hockey and soon made the club and provincial sides. I was also elected as head boy of my school, Suncrest High, which was a great personal milestone, given the fact that only a few years earlier I had been an outsider, a youngster from Poland who couldn't even speak or write English or Afrikaans.

At the age of 16, I joined Waldek as a waitron and later as a barman at Stonehaven, a wedding and conference venue on the banks of the Vaal River, the largest tributary of the Orange River and the third-longest river in South Africa. Stonehaven also catered for the locals in the Vaal area, so there was a great mix of clientele. This brought in much-needed pocket money and gave us some independence while teaching us the value of not squandering what we had worked so hard for.

Waldek and I learnt to become independent at a very early age. Even back in Poland, both my mom and dad worked, so Waldek and I had to fend for ourselves after school until our parents returned home from work. We had a lot of friends; hence our days were spent cycling, playing soccer, fishing, or doing other fun-filled activities. There was no studying or homework being done; this we did later in the evening when our parents got home.

We continued to work at Stonehaven for a number of years to fund our tertiary education, sports, and social activities. The hours were very long. Often, we only finished around 3 am. The experience I gained from my stint as a barman at Stonehaven was invaluable. I learnt how to engage with different people in order to ensure that everyone had a positive customer experience. This is easy when all is going well but harder and more important to achieve when things are not going well.

My work duties also gave me the exposure and ability to speak to people whom I thought were of a more prestigious class than that of my own. This enabled me to see what people outside of my circle were like, to engage with them, and finally to form a view of what I wanted and could achieve in my life. I came to understand that status or money do not make another person better.

I also worked at Checkers, a large supermarket group, and at the bar of the J&B Driving Range, and even did house-sitting to earn extra money.

Our parents had limited money to pay for Waldek and I to go

to university after we matriculated, so we had to fund our own studies. Both of us chose to study at North-West University's Vaal Campus.

My dad had a formula for how much he would contribute towards our tertiary education. He paid for our first year's tuition, which in those days was around R10 000, and then we were on our own. My mother insisted we get a degree of some sort, and she would nag my dad every evening if we weren't studying towards that goal. So my dad, to stop the nagging, forced us to study for a degree. He didn't care what studies we were working towards so long as he could inform my mom we were studying.

My qualification, a BCom Honours in Money and Banking (Economics), which I got cum laude, served me well, and I was soon employed by one of the big banks in South Africa. With a steady and improved source of income, I could continue with my studies.

I joined Standard Bank of South Africa Limited's Corporate and Investment Banking Division in 2002 as Operational Risk Manager, just after completing my degree.

I progressed very well in my banking career and, in 2007, while employed with the bank, was able to get my Master's in Economics through the University of the Witwatersrand.

The following year, I was promoted to the position of Senior Manager, Operational Risk Management within the Corporate and Investment Banking Division of Standard Bank. This was the position I held when I had the accident.

11

A FEW DAYS
BEFORE THE
ACCIDENT

It started with an arbitrary event in April 2010.

Eruptions of the Eyjafjallajökull volcano in Iceland in 2010 caused a cloud of volcanic ash to travel towards Ireland, the United Kingdom, and Europe. Many European countries closed their airspace for fear of the ash damaging or shutting down aircraft engines. This resulted in the biggest air-traffic shutdown since the Second World War. As a result, millions of passengers were stranded, not only in Europe, but also across the world. Many countries, including South Africa, were affected as flights to, from, and over Europe were cancelled.

I didn't know it then, but this force of nature altered the course of my life.

To begin with, I was scheduled to fly to London for business purposes over the forthcoming weekend. I was to meet up with my boss, who was already in London, and to attend a series of work meetings and events.

As the news filtered through that my flight to Heathrow had been cancelled, I found that I needed to reschedule my trip to a more appropriate time. This sudden cancellation not only had an impact on my international business arrangements, but it also meant I had to reorganise my life and my local working plans.

I then realised that the forthcoming Tuesday, 27 April 2010, was a public holiday in South Africa known as "Freedom Day", an annual celebration of the country's first non-racial democratic elections of 1994. This day commemorates the end of more than 300 years of colonialism, segregation, and white-minority rule. It also celebrates the establishment, in 1994, of a new democratic government that was led by Nelson Mandela and that would be subject to a new Constitution.

The banks and many businesses would be closed on that day. As I would've been in London on the Monday, and I'd already cleared my busy schedule at the bank to undertake this trip, I could actually enjoy a long weekend and only needed to return to work later on during the week. It was a wonderful opportunity for meeting up with my brothers and to organise something to do with them on that Monday.

The schools would be closed for a midterm break until Wednesday the week after the following one, so Adrian would be free to fit in with our plans. I convinced Waldek, who was a partner in an auditing/accounting business, to also take the day off on Monday, 26 April 2010, so that us three siblings could enjoy some bonding time and plan things to do over the next few days.

That Monday morning, while Waldek, Adrian, and I were preparing for our cycling trip, my mom said she had a bad premonition and that we shouldn't go cycling at all. Mom often had these feelings, but if we had to listen to her each and every time, we would never leave the house.

We were faced with a choice of riding on the roads in Johannesburg or driving out to cycle somewhere in a reserve or a safe environment.

There had been many reports in South Africa of cyclists being robbed of their bicycles and belongings or knocked over by negligent drivers. Given the fact that Adrian was with us, we decided to take the safer option and rather ride at Suikerbosrand, which has various cycling routes that are ideal for biking. We opted for one of the conventional cycling courses that is about 65 kilometres in length.

We arrived at Suikerbosrand fairly early in the morning and started cycling about 15 minutes later. It was a beautiful, mild day, perfect for a long and enjoyable cycle.

Was it not ironic: we'd made a decision to cycle at Suikerbosrand, a secluded and safe nature reserve, as we deemed it safer than the streets of Johannesburg, yet, from here I was being airlifted to hospital in a critical condition, fighting for my life.

PART III

REGAINING
CONSCIOUSNESS

12

COMING OUT OF
A COMA

It was Mother's Day, 9 May 2010.

I remember seeing lightness and something white. In time, as my eyes adjusted, I realised that I was staring at a white hospital ceiling and its lights. I'm not sure whether this was the first, the tenth, or the hundredth time that I'd woken up, as I was too medicated at that stage to make much sense of it.

My body ached. There was pain everywhere, throbbing throughout my body – my ribs, my knee, my hands, my head, my face, my back, my left shoulder. At times, the pain was so severe, and then … it would seemingly taper off, probably from the next dose of medicine, only to start the vicious cycle of pain all over again.

As my mind drifted in and out of consciousness, I was a bit delirious at times due to the medication and sedatives I received, and I battled to comprehend the situation I now found myself in.

I became aware of sounds, the bleeping of the monitor displaying my vital signs (heart rate and rhythm, blood pressure, and respiratory rate), and the *grrrr* of the ventilator that was supporting my breathing, forcing air into my lungs through a tube inserted into my windpipe. There were feeding tubes, infusion pumps, and some other tubes and pipes leading from my body to different apparatuses, or perhaps it was the other way around and they led from the apparatuses to my body.

Where was this place? What had happened to me?

Now and again, I would see a strange face, an apparition in white peering into my face, touching my body, and then writing something on a chart at the foot of the bed. There were other strange faces that appeared every now and again, and then, as I focused, I recognised the loving faces of my parents, brothers, my sister-in-law, and my girlfriend, Alexandra.

Recognising these familiar and knowing faces brought much relief to me; it brought peace to my soul.

I could see from their expressions that they were overjoyed to see me awake and alive!

I noticed tears in my mother's eyes and looks of concern on the faces of my family and my girlfriend. I cannot recall if there were tears in my eyes. My face was so swollen, and my eyes had sunk into a balloon-like frame.

I tried to reach out to my mom but couldn't; my hands were tied to the bed. I tried to speak to my family but no sound could escape. My face was so badly damaged and my nose was so broken that I had a tracheostomy tube inserted into my throat to help me breathe. I was locked into my body, my world. I couldn't communicate to my loved ones or to the outside world.

This to me was one of those most-dramatic realisations that my world had crumbled and that I was hanging onto life by a thread. What had happened to cause me to end up in this situation?

I could sense my family talking to me, and from their body language and expressions, there was concern through a forced smile or a certain look in their eyes. They couldn't connect with me. They spoke to me but there was no reply emanating from my lips. I thought I could register some of what they said, but not a lot.

As time passed, and as I drifted into and out of consciousness, I recognised other familiar faces; those of my friends, colleagues from my work, and that of Father Jankowski. During this time of semi-consciousness, I realised I was not alone in this room with white lights; there were sounds from the machines and monitors giving life to other patients around me.

I also heard snippets of conversations: some between family, others between medical staff, and even some between visitors and patients near me. It was like I was in a dream, as if I was a person dozing and waking, unsure what was reality or nightmare.

Some of the remarks – not those made by family members but by others at my bedside – were not encouraging about my condition or chances of survival.

The professor heading the team of doctors attending to my recovery was non-committal in his updates and reporting back to my family. While I can understand that he has probably dealt with so many cases during his career, that many of these didn't have the desired outcome, and that he would rather err on the side of caution than get people's hopes up, my personal take on it is that non-committal updates by doctors can leave the patient's family feeling empty or depressed.

On another occasion, there was a group of students standing at the foot of my bed and speaking to Waldek. Having examined my chart and given me the once-over, one of them quite audibly and emphatically stated, "No one can survive this condition."

Those words from that student as well as from those who made similar or negative comments about my condition or chances of survival, unwillingly opened up a door to those demons in my head.

Here I was, fighting for survival, fighting for my life, and looking for signs from the doctors and my family that I was doing okay. At times, I believe I did recognise those signals, and as my hopes were raised, they were also dashed by someone's reaction or comment. One's mindset and attitude are the most important drivers a person can have. This yo-yo effect did not help me and sent confusing messages to the mind, the most powerful tool in one's recovery.

One of the doctors told my family how important it was to remain positive and upbeat when around my bedside and especially when communicating, either to me or among themselves. I am sure that the same message was communicated to the medical and hospital staff, with most living the spirit of the words. There were obviously some exceptions, and I do wish that everyone realised how important their words, looks of encouragement, actions, body language, tone, and expressions were during these delicate stages of life.

One of the most supportive people was Doctor Michelle – I cannot for the life of me recall her surname. However, I later discovered that a family member of hers had experienced a life-changing injury, and that somehow, I reminded her of this person and his circumstances. For me, it was comforting to have engagement with people from the outside world. Receiving some acts of warmth and encouragement also helped to allay some of the demons in my head.

13

THE FIRST FEW DAYS AFTER AWAKING FROM A COMA

The days seemingly passed, and here and there people appeared at my bedside.

I had no way of knowing the time or what day it was aside from seeing my family arrive in a change of clothes and the nursing staff change shifts.

There were always the familiar faces of my parents around me. My mother, Dana, was there every time I looked out for support and love. Often, I would see my dad, Frank, in the ward, supporting and comforting my mom and encouraging me in his own way. Seeing them both around me certainly cemented our bond and brought us much closer through this terrible ordeal.

In those first days that followed my regaining of consciousness, I experienced a great deal of frustration, especially in trying to communicate with my loved ones or the doctors to find out what was going on with me. I, however, didn't need to hear the words; their facial expressions and body language spoke to me loud enough. I was in trouble.

My ability to communicate was largely compromised. However, as the days passed, I became a little bit more attuned to my surroundings and what people were saying to me. I gathered that the patients near me in the ICU ward were survivors of trauma and they too were locked into their body and mind to various degrees. They were also unable or struggling to communicate with their loved ones or with the outside world. In all my 30 years until this moment, I had not realised the magnitude of this debilitating situation.

How many hundreds of thousands of people in the world have found themselves in a similar situation; those with Alzheimer's, or stroke or accident survivors? And what about those prone to seizures, others who experience oxygen deprivation due to cardiac arrest, those who have near-drowning incidents, or diabetics who go into a comatose state?

The conditions that cause people to go into a coma don't only afflict the elderly. They affect babies, children, and adults as well. A person's life, like mine did, can change in seconds.

I heard of a case where a young child went into hospital for an appendix operation, slipped in the ward, and ended up in a coma. These things happen in the blink of an eye and yet can take people years to recover from, if they recuperate at all.

I also know of a situation, much closer to home, where the head of a family suffered a stroke. At first, the entire family thought that he would recover quickly, but as days went by he started slipping further and further away. In the end, he passed away, but it seemed to me that his family wasn't willing to fight on his behalf. That is the part that really upset me and was the opposite to my family's reaction, unconditional support, love, and prayers.

I learnt later that my mother visited me every day from 6 am until 10 pm, at which point the nurses and medical staff begged her to go home to rest. For 16 hours a day, every day without fail, my mother was at my side, talking to me, praying for me, encouraging and supporting me. But it was not only my mom; the rest of my close family – my dad, Waldek, Pauline, Adrian, and Alexandra – all sacrificed their personal time, in between school, jobs, and life to come and support and visit me.

Alexandra had her own child, and Waldek had his own family, including a one-month-old baby who demanded his attention. Later in my recovery, friends, and colleagues from work were allowed short visits. These certainly gave me the will to live, and I am very appreciative of them. There is no doubt these visits and personal sacrifices of my loved ones, and the intercession of all the prayers offered on my behalf, had a profound impact on my ultimate recovery.

In the days that passed since I came out of my induced coma, I started to understand some of the events that had unfolded since the service vehicle smashed into me on that hill in Suikerbosrand.

I was told that I'd been in an induced coma for 14 days and gave my mom a wonderful gift by returning, albeit very partially, to the world on 9 May 2010, which was Mother's Day.

My family was able to tell me about parts of the accident and, over time I began to put the dots together and appreciate the chain of events and what had happened when I was knocked into unconsciousness.

Adrian and Waldek were cycling ahead of me. A couple of kilometres into the journey, we were ascending a hill; my two brothers were positioned ten metres ahead and to the right of me. They couldn't see the peak of the hill, as the road curved quite sharply to our left.

Suddenly, out of nowhere and without warning, a service vehicle came speeding from the opposite direction, around the bend we were approaching. It was a single cab, white, with an open back, a work vehicle, owned by the reserve and operated by one of its employees. It was speeding at approximately 90 kilometres per hour and was heading straight for Adrian and Waldek.

At the last second, the vehicle swerved out of their path and went straight into me.

My hands hit the bonnet first, my left knee hit the lights, causing severe lacerations, and my body made contact with the vehicle's hood, which fractured my ribs and shattered my shoulder. Thereafter, my head went through the windshield and made contact with the steering wheel, which resulted in a broken nose and jaw, broken cheekbones, as well as numerous cracks in my skull, the shifting of my left eye backwards, and the degloving of my face.

I learnt how providence played its part and that Mr Nigel Henderson had just happened to be at the Protea Hotel at that very moment, to help and stabilise me while waiting for the emergency services to arrive. My blessing resulted from Nigel and his new bride's misfortune; the same volcanic eruption which resulted in me cycling that day resulted in this couple being unable to leave South Africa as originally planned.

My family also elaborated on Waldek's mad dash to get me to the Protea Hotel to find assistance, Adrian's heroic work to keep my face on my body and his fingers in my mouth to stop me choking to death, and me being airlifted to the hospital. I was also filled in about the past weeks of my life lying strapped to a bed in the ICU ward to prevent me from falling off from involuntary convulsions, fighting for life and survival.

14

TAKING STOCK OF MY BROKEN BODY

It was three weeks since the accident and only a week since coming out of the coma.

I couldn't recall anything about the accident, and even to this day it is a void in my memory banks. I also don't recall too much about the time I was in the coma, but I do believe I heard messages and people speaking to me. I also remember the powerful and uplifting lyrics of my favourite band, Pearl Jam, playing in my ears. I later learnt that Waldek had inserted earphones into my ears while I was in a coma, and had played my favourite songs to me each and every day.

I was now at the stage of taking stock of the extent of the injuries I had incurred and the situation in which I found myself.

Someone held a mirror close to my face so I could take a look at myself. I couldn't recognise the face I was staring at. My head was still severely swollen, but apparently it was much less so than had been the case during the first couple of nights after the accident when my family witnessed first-hand the damage caused by the incident. My ears were hardly visible, and my eyes were still somewhat sunken into my swollen head. Half of my hair was replaced by staples which ran from my left ear, over the top of my head, to my right ear. I felt like a combination of Pinhead from *Hellraiser*, given my bald head and staples, and Neo from *The Matrix*, with pipes connected to my body. And, to top it all off, I was wearing a diaper and was strapped to the bed.

This was a huge jolt to me and I could then fathom what a shock it must've been for my family, Alexandra, friends, and colleagues to see me like this. And what about the doctors and nursing staff? I happened to glimpse a picture of me, taken a few months before the accident and which was neatly placed on the bedside table, beside a bunch of flowers and get-well cards. My picture was flanked by others, of Jesus on the one side, and of Mary, the Mother of Jesus, on the other.

It was upsetting to see the transformation and utter deterioration in my physical appearance. I was told that my mother had placed that photo of me next to my hospital bed in order to humanise me, as my appearance was monstrous to some of the hospital staff. She wanted them to know that her son was indeed human and not a blob in a broken body.

My hands were swollen and bruised. My left hand looked deformed, with some of the knuckles having moved back, causing the carpals (the bones of the wrist) and metacarpals (the five bones of the hand) to rise about four centimetres from their original position. This would require corrective surgery.

I had problems with my eyes: I couldn't focus or control them and at times I looked at things or people rather squinty. My right eye is more damaged due to injury to the right optic nerve and still causes me issues even today. For example, when I watch television or work on a computer, I need to place my hand over my right eye to block out the sight from the damaged eye. The injury has left me with a permanent blind spot.

My knees, particularly my right one, were severely damaged by the impact with the vehicle, so much so that I was unable to walk. This issue was not of immediate concern to the doctors, whose main priority was to stabilise my condition and ensure I survived the ordeal. It was only much later that the full extent of my leg and knee injuries became known.

Dr Michael Laric was the orthopaedic surgeon who attended to me and was responsible for operating on my shoulder and on my damaged hand. He told my family I was too young to live with an artificial limb so he would do his best to save my arm and shoulder. It did however necessitate a major operation and again titanium was inserted to hold that part of my anatomy together. He is a great doctor and I am extremely grateful to him for the work done on my body.

However, despite therapy and continual exercise, I have never regained the full movement of my left shoulder and arm.

The titanium plates inserted into my face around the nasal area, jaw, and eye sockets were causing severe discomfort, and infection resulted. This meant I underwent another operation to reduce the number of plates holding my sinus passage and mouth region together.

The joke in the family was that I would set off every metal detector I went through and would be body-searched. I do have to admit that although this was a family joke, I was somewhat concerned that it may come true. Fortunately, this was not to be the case!

I also had much pain in and many problems with my back; the diagnosis was that I had four compressed discs and eight of my vertebrae were fractured. I would have to wear a brace continuously for about four months from my neck down to my waist to support my back. On top of that, I sustained a left lung contusion and four fractured ribs; this is where I developed a chronic dislike of sneezing. Every time I sneezed, it felt like millions of pins were being shot into my chest. Given the fierce impact, I also suffered abdominal injury with laceration of the upper pole of the right kidney.

In all, I had about seven operations and what felt like tons of titanium plates inserted into my body.

As though this wasn't bad enough, I learnt that I'd suffered significant trauma to the head, with multiple skull fractures and soft-tissue injuries.

The multiple skull fractures included those to the left frontal sinus, left temporal, left parietal, right occipital, and left and right frontal bones.

I had sustained a severe diffuse brain injury, which implied that multiple areas of the brain were affected. After this type of brain injury, the majority of patients retain long-term cognitive and personality changes.

There was bone fragment displaced into the frontal lobe on the left side as well as a large subdural left haematoma (when blood collects between the skull and the surface of the brain) with midline shift (when swelling and blood build-up cause the whole brain to shift off-centre) and cerebral oedema (a life-threatening inflammatory reaction). There was displacement of the cortical sulci (the depressions or grooves in the folded surface of grey matter) and the basal cisterns (spaces formed by openings in the membranes that envelop the brain and spinal cord).

A craniotomy was performed to treat the subdural haematoma, which implied the surgical removal of part of the skull bone to allow for the draining of the blood.

Given the physical and brain injuries, one possible outcome was that I would be in a vegetative state, in diapers and requiring 24/7 nursing. Another, better outlook for me, was that I would never walk again, and would be confined to a wheelchair, with potentially severe brain damage.

How quickly things can change in a person's life; in the blink of an eye. One minute, I had everything going for me. An excellent and high-level job, a beautiful girlfriend, a wonderful family, many great friends … and then within a split second I was in a coma, lying bound in a bed in the ICU ward of Union Hospital.

I was alive, but physically, mentally, and spiritually, I was in a bad way, mainly due to the pain. I realised I had a long, long road ahead of me and it was not going to be easy. I would have to call on every bit of my strength of character to get me through. But, at least I had a start; I had already survived three weeks of hell.

15

GRUNGE
INSPIRATION

As mentioned earlier, Waldek used to insert earphones into my ears each and every day and play some of my favourite Pearl Jam songs. These included, among others, "Down", "Fatal", and "I'm the Ocean" (the last song is from an album by Neil Young, featuring Pearl Jam).

What I love about Pearl Jam, apart from the brilliant grunge music, and the rocking lyrics, is the fact that they don't divulge the meaning of their songs. They empower their fans to interpret them to derive their own unique meaning, given their specific situation and emotional state. Pearl Jam has had an effect on me from my teens, and I guess their lyrics always subconsciously influenced my life, just as they did when I was stuck in a coma. Without me realising it, they put the fire back into me.

I'm not entirely sure whether I recall the music from when I was still in the coma or from when my mind was drifting between consciousness and unconsciousness after I awoke from it. But I do know one thing for sure: of the abovementioned favourite songs, "Down" was the one that had the biggest impact on me.

While I can't reproduce the lyrics here due to copyright reasons, I encourage you to look them up online and to listen to the song.

Given the situation I was in and my state of mind, this is how I interpreted the lyrics of the song:

> I am down. I have been left by the wayside while the world carries on. I am trapped in this damaged body with no way of getting out.
> I am down. I have cried about it for such a long time that my tears can no longer be seen. This is of no use.
> I can pretend to be someone else, but my situation remains the same.
> I am enraged but that's all for nothing. Help me control myself.
>
> Rise. Everyone is alive but I am stuck in the same place.
> Rise. I can't just do nothing, while the whole world carries on.
> One day my pain will fade. I will not wait, and I'll rather throw the pain pills away.
> And if a man who is hurt like me can find hope, so can everyone else.
>
> I will not allow the life to escape from me.
> I will not allow death and this broken body to swallow me.

This still chokes me up with tears. If you are the family member of anyone who finds themself trying to recover from a traumatic situation or if you are the injured person, look to music to bring comfort, reduce anxiety, to inspire, and to be a beacon of hope.

16

A MOTHER'S LOVE, AND HER FAITH AND TRUST IN GOD

There is something special about a mother's love and bond with her children.

It's even more special when a mother's love is coupled with a mother's deep faith and belief in God. Then I believe a child is truly blessed.

My mother was and still is a very devout Catholic. My dad went to church occasionally, but that changed the night of the accident. Adrian told me how my dad got down on his knees and forced all family members to follow his example and to join in, as a family, in prayer for my life and recovery. Sometimes tragedies and certain events in the family do bring people closer to God.

I have mentioned how my mom stayed with me, 16 hours a day every day since the accident, while I was in hospital. My mom would leave home in the dark and get home late at night in the dark. The South African winter was approaching, and while the days were temperate, the nights became very cold. Father Jankowski visited me very often, almost daily, would give me a special pastoral blessing, and together with my mom would pray over me.

It was very fitting and symbolic to me that while this was taking place on Mother's Day, 9 May 2010, I began to come around from my comatose state. Although I was in an induced coma, there was a high degree of uncertainty whether or not I would open my eyes again.

My mom tells me that I initially made a sound or two, and then very briefly opened my eyes. One does not just wake up from a coma at a snap of the fingers, as if you were under a hypnotist's spell. My mom apparently got such a fright, she thought it was my death rattle and ran to summon the nursing staff to come help me. The nurse on duty recognised the signs and broke the wonderful news to those at the bedside that I was coming around from my shadowed world and into the light.

It was enough for everyone to be overjoyed. A miracle had taken place. With my mother's love and the blessing and grace of God, I'd made it through the worst storm of my life. The road ahead would still be hard, but there was hope, there was light at the end of the journey. Sometimes that is all a person needs in life.

17

THE PAIN
THRESHOLD

Pain changes and pain changes a person.

The one thing I recall to this day is the intense pain I experienced after coming around from my induced coma. I continue to experience some of this pain today.

At first, it was a physical phenomenon and my entire body was hurting. It can be likened to a nagging tooth abscess, throbbing continuously, but not emitting from one part of the body but from the entire body. Day and night the pain endures. It is, however, not one of those sensations like a tooth abscess that dulls over time and in fact disappears once the abscess drains or the antibiotics take effect.

The pain, especially in my shoulder, was severe.

It was not the first time I'd injured my shoulder or had come, good and proper, off my bicycle. My mind flashed back to when I was about seven years of age, riding my bicycle in our village of Wojkowice Kościelne. Together with a couple of friends, I would cycle in the street where we lived. They stayed up the road from me, and the ground sloped upwards, so it was always fun riding downhill back home.

We used to have a gate at the entrance to our home, but it was broken and stayed ajar in a certain position, neither fully opened nor closed. Usually, when returning home from my friends, I would cycle down the hill and negotiate the turn into our front garden by steering the bicycle through the posts and broken gate. One time, I came down the hill really fast and when trying to go through the gate, I crashed into the gatepost, breaking my collarbone.

Strangely enough, I was placed in plaster of Paris from the waist to the neck. What made it worse is that one gets itchy under the plaster and I recall the frustration I felt to scratch my armpits. The only consolation I had when wearing the body armour of plaster of Paris was that when I played football with my friends, I became the best goalie ever, because I would just stand in the goals and when the guys would shoot, I'd defend with my chest and armour-plated bulletproof vest.

Similar to the plaster of Paris cast I had to wear in my youth, the brace I now had to wear fitted around my torso, from my neck to my waist. At least I could loosen the brace or take it off when I had a bed bath or needed to scratch an itch.

But it was the pain that was the biggest hurdle. This type of pain prevents one from sleeping and is an insurmountable challenge to one's mindset and belief system on the road to a recovery and an improvement of one's lifestyle.

If I had to compare the pain to, say, the magnitude of an earthquake measured on the Richter Scale, it would range from an eight to a ten, depending on when the medication kicked in and wore off. Generally, people have a high or low threshold for pain. I would say I have a very high one, yet still every day was characterised by extreme and consistent pain for me.

One never knows how a person will react in any given set of circumstances. This is not only applicable to pain but also to overcoming adversity and some of life's most horrendous events and/or injustices.

What about those brave souls who survived the horrors of concentration camps, were tortured and spent years as prisoners-of-war? It wasn't their calling or personal decision to be there but they had to pay the ultimate price of being a pawn in someone else's vision or as a result of having to defend their land and family from invaders.

18

FIGHTING FOR SURVIVAL

The beast, a lion, charged at me.

My mind, mainly due to the effects of the medication, continued to slip between consciousness and unconsciousness. My only real memory of this time of semi-consciousness is of a vivid dream, or perhaps rather of a nightmare, in which I was engaged in a battle, fighting for my life against one of the fiercest cats and predators in nature, a lion.

I can't recall many dreams I had in hospital or even if I dreamt much. However, this one I recollect vividly. I remember a lion slowly stalking me. Then suddenly, the beast rose up on its hind legs, and then, swinging with its front paws, it made contact with me, cutting my abdomen into six slices. I began to fall apart, like something out of a cartoon for children. I was face to face with the lion with all its pride, ugliness, and ferocity.

At that moment, I raised up my arms and started to scream as loud as I could at the beast. At first, this had no effect. So I raised my voice and started to run towards the lion, screaming and moving my hands above my head like a crazy person. This no doubt startled the giant animal that then turned and, with its tail between its legs, left me in peace.

To me, this dream represented my body and mind fighting for survival. I was initially so thankful that what I'd just envisioned had not happened in reality and came to the conclusion that there was, in fact, a much deeper and more meaningful message within my subconscious. I was in control of my destiny, my recovery, my life. I could not abdicate this responsibility to anyone else. But I needed to act, decisively. I had to put away those demons in my head and the pain I was going through and concentrate on living, one day at a time.

Interestingly, and unbeknown to me, Ewa Sarnecka, my cousin Iza Milewska's friend from Poland, heard about my accident. At the time, Ewa was visiting some of the holy sites and shrines in Jerusalem, and she volunteered to offer her prayers for me during her travels. It was during this time that Ewa had a dream or a vision very similar to mine. In fact, she witnessed me fighting off a black panther, and she sent word back to South Africa to reassure the family that I was fighting for my life and winning the battle.

These two dreams, or visions, were experienced virtually simultaneously by two different people many miles apart. How uncanny! Was there a special message in this?

Will I die or live? I thought. *What will happen if I die today? Have I fulfilled my dreams and purpose in my life? What is my purpose in life? I am only 30 years of age ... surely I am too young to die?*

Death has no time limit. It comes like a thief in the night. It comes for babies, the aged, and everyone in between. In fact, death is a certainty in life that is going to happen to each and every one of us. Are we prepared for that fate?

The first time I encountered death was as a youngster back in Poland. I must have been around six or seven years of age. My friend's brother was crossing the main road, a double-lane one that connected our village to large towns in the north and south of Poland, when he was tragically hit by a car and died at the scene.

This was extremely traumatic to me and my friends. Death had come very close to us. My friend and his family were devastated. The community, a small and closely-knit bunch of people, was grief-stricken. I was young but very impressionable. It hit me very hard. I knew the boy and his family very well. Waldek and I crossed that same road often. It could have happened to us.

Waldek and I served as altar boys at my friend's brother's funeral. The boy's family sat in the front row and was heartbroken. His mom cried throughout the service. My friend looked so lost, so desolate … slumped in the bench next to his mom. We also had to walk in front of the priest and the coffin from the church to the graveyard, and again we witnessed such emotional and upsetting scenes, especially the lowering of the coffin into the grave.

That same scene I relived from my childhood would play out again in my current circumstances. My family would be sitting in the front row of the church devastated and broken. My mom sobbing uncontrollably. My friends and colleagues would also be grief-stricken.

What would they be saying about me? About the life I had lived until now. How had I made an impact on their lives or the world in general? It was motivation enough to pull through and survive. Besides, I had a lot more to offer people and society in this life.

I realised that this boy and I had something in common besides our background in Poland. We both got hit by a vehicle. Unfortunately, he passed away and I lived.

In fact, I believe in retrospection; my dream of me fighting the lion was one of the very important factors that broke the yo-yo effect of my recovery and made me want to grab and hold onto life with all my might.

19

WOULD SOŁTYS STILL BE PROUD OF ME?

There was another inner struggle raging inside of me. Regardless of whether my inner strength was wavering from the physical pain or the mental anguish from the doubts that swirled around in my head like a swarm of bees, my mind continuously focused on my loving grandfather, who was living thousands of miles away in Poland.

And often, throughout the day, I would default to the same question, "Would my grandfather be proud to call me his grandson should he see me now?"

I feared that in most cases the answer would be "No".

My grandfather was a winner, not a quitter. I have already mentioned how he survived the horrors of war and a German camp and then how he provided for his family and community after the war. He was my hero and role model. Now I was scared I was letting him down.

On reflection, I was perhaps foolish to question this, because we'd spent enough time together for me to know that he would've been proud of me regardless. However, deep down inside, I didn't want to disrespect his name by giving up too easily, or by seeing myself as a man around whom the whole world revolved. If that was the case, then there would've been no one living a tougher life than me; no one who in fact might've been hit even harder than I was by a car; no one who'd had some other misfortune worse than mine befall them.

I realised that I was better off than some and worse off than others, like we all are in this world, so to shed tears over my own circumstances would've been a useless exercise. Instead, I focused on the hardships I knew my grandfather endured, and I kept persevering in my attempts to recover.

This thought, I believe, was another turning point in my recovery; it subconsciously empowered me to define the identity of the man I wanted to be. I was not going to be the victim of some careless driver's actions.

I made a decision: *I am a fighter. I am not going to quit on life.*

In the days that followed my return to the world, my loved ones were told that my survival rate had improved to below 10%. The odds had doubled since my earlier prognosis while lying in a vegetative state.

PART IV

MY CHALLENGES AND
THE ROAD TO RECOVERY

20

HOPE

In search of further sources of inspiration, I turned to the most unlikely of places, the Lance Armstrong "Livestrong" wristband.

Prior to my accident, I was never fond of Armstrong, to say the least, hence Waldek's silly idea to put the band on my wrist while I was in a coma. I appreciated his corny sense of humour; at first, I was unable to remove it, as I was strapped to the bed, but later I decided to keep it on, just for the heck of it, never expecting the immense sense of motivation it would deliver.

My dislike of Armstrong started long before his drug scandal or the rumours that he was using steroids to enhance his performance. Something just didn't tie up: he was winning, had a strong competitive spirit/attitude, defeated cancer, and was undertaking philanthropic work through the Livestrong cancer foundation ... yet he spoke to and treated people like he was aiming to win the arse of the century award. The competition for which was fierce, with Juventus Football Club – which was found to have rigged games in the 2004–05 and 2005–06 Italian Serie A seasons – and Russian Olympians – of whom 20 were stripped of their Olympic medals by 2010 – being firm favourites.

However, despite my dislike, I ended up drawing immense inspiration from those two words on the wristband, "live" and "strong", to refocus my energy and determination to recover from my dreadful situation. And at times, when the pain throughout my body was unbearable, my mind grabbed hold of those two words which allowed me to push myself further through the pain threshold, until my end goal became visible again and the cloud of doubt that filled my mind disappeared.

While I didn't have cancer, I knew that there were many people in this world suffering some sort of trauma, regardless of its origin.

Here was the start of an idea that formulated in my head. If I could survive this horrific ordeal, having been given a less-than 5% chance of making it, then I too could pass my philosophies and hope on to others.

This idea was the start of my newfound purpose in life. It also became clearer to me the reason why I had survived the accident and regained consciousness from the coma. My life's journey, and particularly the recovery from my accident, could now serve as a living testimony to others and give them hope for their future.

21

ALL THIS PAIN JUST TO PUT ON A SOCK

To regain some humanity and dignity, I undertook the task of learning how to sit and walk again.

I'd been lying in the ICU bed for about five weeks; now it was time to get mobile again. Owing to my immobility, I was peeing through a pipe, which was causing me quite a lot of discomfort. At one stage, I was briefly thankful to my brother, who decided to remove it to ease my discomfort; however, my happiness was swiftly washed away as urine poured out of the pressurised pipe and onto my bed and my body.

I needed to be able to go to the bathroom by myself. And then there was the long-term goal I set for myself. I desperately wanted to ride my bicycle again. Contrary to what happens to so many people when an accident befalls them, I didn't want to become fearful of and stop the activity I was doing when the accident happened. I've heard of cases where people, after falling off a bicycle or a horse, or being involved in a car accident or nearly drowning, shy away from riding, driving, or swimming for the rest of their lives and in a sense never truly recover from the trauma. That was not going to happen to me.

There was also a bigger picture: I needed to be able to drive again, to work, to be able to get on a plane and travel, in essence to live a normal life or as close to a normal life as possible. I also wanted to get married and have children.

Once I made up my mind to regain my independence, it took me a couple of days to be able to lift myself up into a seated position, with each attempt resulting in severe pain, defeat, and anguish ... after which I pulled myself together in order to attempt the task again and again. Of course, I had to make sure I didn't do any further damage to my shoulder or the plates holding the joints in position.

Some family members have said I am quite stubborn. I'm not sure if I agree with them, but I am driven and focused, and if I say I am going to do a thing, I do it. It is this determination, stubbornness, and focus that has got me through my ordeal to date, and it's these characteristics and values that will get me to the next stage.

Once I was able to lift myself into a seated position, I attempted the next challenge, which was to walk by myself.

This proved to be harder than expected due to the injury to my right knee. I couldn't bend it very much and I wasn't able to put on a sock or to wash my foot. And the pain was excruciating.

At this stage of my recovery, I was moved to a general ward in the hospital, and was now sharing a room with five other patients, each of whom had their own challenges and their own journeys to recovery.

The doctors diagnosed the reason for me not being able to walk as a condition called calcification, which simply means the accumulation of calcium salts in body tissue. This process was initiated by my body as a healing mechanism due to all of the broken bones; my body was literally trying to glue itself back together. This was of course good in places where the bones were in fact broken and needed to be glued, but it wasn't such a good thing in my right knee, as there were no major fractures there. This resulted in an additional bone formation on the side of my knee, into which the medial collateral ligament (the MCL – a band of tissue along the inner edge of the knee) had been glued.

My doctors gave me two options:

Option one was to wait for four years for the calcification process to end, and to then have an operation.

Option two was to tear off the ligament from the new bone. Initially, option two sounded like the best one because, although it sounded painful, I thought I could achieve it in one sitting and was willing to push through the pain.

However, the doctor further explained that it wasn't that simple, as I would have to tear off a bit of the ligament every day until the calcification process ended. It would be naturally re-glued overnight, and then I would repeat the process of tearing the re-glued piece and a bit more the following day to make some progress.

As the calcification process slowed down over time, the tearing-off business would become increasingly easier ...

All this pain just to put on a sock or to wash my own foot.

I decided on option two.

22

WHAT WE SAY
TO OURSELVES
IN THE MIRROR

After a stay of about two months in Union Hospital, of which approximately five weeks were in ICU and three weeks in a general ward, I was moved to a step-down facility, in Milpark, which catered for the rehabilitation of patients with trauma similar to what I'd experienced.

Part of my rehab was to do certain daily exercises to get my legs moving and to bend my knee a little more than I'd been able to before. Often, I initiated these activities of my own accord outside of the sessions. I knew that the continual therapy would eventually enable me to walk and ride freely again. And so, with that vision of the future, I was prepared, mentally and physically, to endure the torture of these sessions. At times, the pain was still so severe that I thought I might faint from it.

On the odd occasion, I fell flat on my face, but at least I was falling forward. With each fall came a stronger commitment to get up and proceed. I was going to walk freely and unaided again. Slowly, inch by inch, day by day, I could feel the difference, an encouraging improvement in my physical handicap. Despite the agony I had to withstand, there was cause to be optimistic.

I however did not enjoy the brain-therapy sessions and hated the short-term memory games I was subjected to. The therapist would read out a story and then ask questions, following which I would have to reply with all of the story details. At times, I couldn't remember a thing I'd heard. At other times, I was able to recall some facts but thereafter my memory would fade again. I tried my absolute best to change, to remember more, but there was just no improvement.

I'm sure there has been a lot of thought and scientific and medical research into the therapy approach to help brain-injury survivors to recover, but to me, it was a belittling exercise.

Here I was, at age 30 and a banker, having to repeat a very basic paragraph or verse that had been read to me. It reminded me of my time in my early grades at school. To get even the simplest story incorrect or to repeat details incoherently was very demeaning. I would've preferred it if they'd asked me to repeat something far more intricate and difficult, like a paragraph from Karl Marx or Albert Einstein; then I wouldn't have felt so bad.

Fortunately, over time, these sessions became more infrequent; I guess because my memory and inputs were reaching an acceptable level.

Looking back, I guess that my frustration wasn't levelled at the system or the personnel who so diligently pushed and prodded my mind to return to a better functioning level, but at the inability to express the thoughts or pictures in my mind into words, to communicate to others, to express my feelings or needs.

Again, those feelings of inadequacy I had when I first came out of the coma would haunt my thinking and progress. They became little voices of doubt that said to me:

"You are wrong; you are not getting better."

"You cannot even remember some of the basic messages; the shortest of sentences."

"You are a failure."

"You will be incapacitated for the rest of your life."

As I continued looking for hope and encouragement, I realised I had already made a lot of progress on my road to recovery. From almost being a goner, I was now in rehab and undergoing therapy. The strength and input I got from the positive support of my family, listening to music that uplifted my spirit, the Livestrong wristband, and focusing on my grandfather as a role model, were focal points to this shifting mindset. Another immense boost to my confidence and resolve was my attitude and my thought process to not dwell on the pain I was experiencing. If I could just keep going, applying the same focus and determination, there was light for me at the end of the tunnel. There was HOPE!

It's amazing what you can achieve if you focus your efforts, one thought at a time, on a specific goal. In my case, my goal was to get better, and I determined to banish negative thoughts as soon as they entered my mind, and to replace them with thoughts that could build me up and not tear me down.

Funny enough, over time, I came to the realisation that I may have been extremely hard on myself and that for some reason I was trying to recover to a state of perfection, without recognising that I was never perfect to begin with. Although pushing myself was a very good thing, I shouldn't have looked down on my achievements by striving for an unrealistic state of flawlessness. Such actions negatively impacted my recovery. One doesn't have to be perfect in everything he or she does, just like one doesn't have to wait for a perfect time … these things simply don't exist.

Like in anything in life, there is a balancing act on how hard we have to be on ourselves. Yes, we mustn't be lazy, quit, or continually make excuses, but at times, we may actually be harder on ourselves than we are on others. We mustn't make our competitive nature and drive cause us to be our own worst enemy. What do we say to that man or woman in the mirror? How do we treat that person?

Perhaps a little more gentleness, self-love, and acknowledgement of the achievement of the intermediary goals is the recipe for continued improvement and/or personal development. This revelation made a big impact on my mentality.

23

THE PONYTAILED
PSYCHOLOGIST

Am I indeed crazy? Have the two weeks in a coma affected my logic and thinking?

This was what I was mulling over following a question posed to me by a psychologist in one of my therapy sessions. He was an elderly gentleman with a ponytail. In typical psychologist fashion, he wanted to know how I would react today if the incident happened to me, so he asked: "Are you angry at what happened to you on that hill in Suikerbosrand that day; that the car hit you and not someone else?"

I answered immediately, without even considering the question for long, "No, and I would rather the car hit me – not my brothers – again."

My reply astonished and shocked him. His jaw dropped and he stared at me, mouth agape. I wasn't sure if he thought I was the craziest person in the world at that stage or if he was just simply surprised by my reply that perhaps defied the textbooks and experiences he'd encountered to date.

His reaction caught me off guard. And over the next couple of days, my mind would hauntingly replay my answer to the question.

Am I mad? Did my time in a coma affect my answer to what, at first glance, seems a very simple question?

The more I thought about it, the more I realised I'd given the correct response.

I later learnt that the psychologist went to my mom and related his surprise and shock at my answer. He told her that in all his years of practice he'd never had a patient who was *not* irate at the cause of the accident. He confided to her that I didn't blame God for all of my suffering, and that I'd told him that if it were to happen again, I'd rather it was me – and not my brothers – who was hit. He concluded by saying, "I wish I had a brother like that."

It's one of those cases where you play the "what if" game. What if the car had hit Adrian or Waldek? They may've been killed, suffered brain damage, or some dreadful fate. Waldek was a husband and father; the thought of his wife and children being left without their breadwinner and key family member was too terrible to contemplate. Adrian was just a kid of 16 at that time. He had his whole life ahead of him.

My love for my family and particularly my brothers is so great that I would not want them to endure for one minute or hour what I have to contend with on a daily basis.

In hindsight, there is nothing strange about this decision or this kind of love. Every day, parents, spouses, or siblings would do anything in their power to protect or help a loved one. People donate a kidney or other body parts to, give blood to, and wish they could trade places with, a person or family member in need.

I am so fortunate I have a close and loving family.

Yes, like all families, we have our moments. There was a time when Waldek and I would come to physical blows over something so small as a stupid goal that I'd failed to prevent while playing hockey. Our fights would take teammates by surprise. But ten minutes later, Waldek and I would be the best of mates with no grudges or animosity. We were family. Yes, we can be a bit hot-headed at times, but there has always been an underlying love and bond between us that is so special. We have carried this closeness through to Adrian and our extended family.

These days, one is lucky to have a complete family with all parents and siblings still alive, and whose members actually get on with each other. There are so many cases in this world where death, divorce, alcohol, drugs, or wars, have broken down a family. Also pettiness, greed, and the spirit of intolerance and blame have split families such that some members never speak to each other again.

24

FALLING
FORWARD

I didn't enjoy my stay at the rehabilitation centre, and I found the setup, and the morale of the patients quite upsetting. This affected me negatively. Some patients in my ward seemed disengaged, as though they didn't want to fight for their survival, for their recovery. They were seemingly content with their current situation or just happy to give up and die.

The medical aid had recommended this rehab centre. I begged my family to have me moved. Eventually, after about two or three weeks of this anguish, we came to a decision that I be discharged from hospital as a full-time patient and attend the daily rehab sessions as an outpatient. I could stay at my home, which was much better for me than being in any hospital or step-down facility. This arrangement, however, necessitated someone staying with me. My mom was there by my side for about another two months. I was still unable to do everything by myself, so I really needed the help. My memory and my senses were still not where they needed to be. I would forget to eat and would probably have lost a finger or two if I tried to cook. My dad was there as well, but he had to go back to their house from time to time to ensure that all was in order. It was great having him around; his humour and muscles made him a welcome and needed guest.

Given the arrangements, my dad or Waldek or Pauline would need to drive me to rehab every morning, and someone else would have to fetch me later in the day. But it wasn't easy getting to the centre. To begin with, I was kitted out with a brace to support my back, and this made it challenging for me to get in and out of a car. Given my severely compromised back, I wasn't able to sit upright in the car; the pain was simply too excruciating. Waldek had to put the passenger seat down so that I could recline with my back brace firmly attached. Then we had other logistics to contend with: Who would take me to and fetch me from the sessions, given the fact that my family members had their own work and personal commitments to tend to? The Johannesburg traffic was another aggravating aspect.

By this stage in my recovery, I had progressed from being dependent on a wheelchair to move around to now just using crutches. This was a psychological boost to me and a sure sign I was winning the battle. I could visualise being back on the bicycle again. There was hope, there was progress. I had come this far and there was no stopping me. It became a burning desire and focused goal that I walk, cycle, drive, travel, and work again unaided, without crutches, wheelchairs, or walking sticks. Nothing, not the pain, the therapy, the nursing staff and certainly not myself, was going to stop me from achieving this. I was going to make it.

I even looked forward to playing soccer again in the future. During June 2010, while I was still in the hospital, everyone there, and in fact the whole country, waited in anticipation for South Africa to play in the opening game of the FIFA Soccer World Cup. The country was abuzz with excitement, and the unification of all South Africans through sport was a sight to behold. South Africa had won the right to host this prestigious world event. The games were televised worldwide, and tourists flocked to the country. There was a television set in the general ward, and at times I could follow snippets of the games.

The biggest disappointment for me about this World Cup, besides the fact that Poland had failed to qualify for it, was that I wasn't in the stands watching the games being played, soaking up the atmosphere and excitement. I'd intended to take some of my annual leave during the World Cup, and had already bought a number of tickets for games at different stadiums across the country. Now, I was laid up in hospital and had to give the tickets away to family and friends. I could, however, follow the thrilling games from my hospital bed ... but it wasn't the same as being at a live event.

25

MY GOAL
TO RIDE AGAIN

It remained my goal, my dream, my burning desire, to get back on the bicycle and lead a life as near to normal as I possibly could. I knew that if I could pass the bicycle test, of being able to cycle again, I would consider that to be the end point of my recovery.

I was still undergoing intensive therapy when I mentioned to my family and the physiotherapists that I wanted to cycle again. Some of my family members disapproved of the idea out of fear for me, while others supported me 100%.

Waldek then spoke to his friend, who owned a bicycle-distribution shop, to find the right bike for me. Soon, I was the owner of a world-class Cervélo R3. At the time, this bike was used by phenomenal cycling team Garmin–Cervélo in events such as the Paris–Roubaix and the Tour de France. In fact, Johan Vansummeren won the Paris–Roubaix on a Cervélo R3 in 2011. This meant I was serious about my goal. It would ensure I would cycle again and compete in some of South Africa's main cycling events, such as the 94.7 Cycle Challenge on my road bicycle, and the Cape Epic (also known as "The Epic") on my mountain bike.

I placed the new bicycle in my room in full view of my bed and chair. I needed to see it every day. This is an important aspect for dreams or goals to come to fruition. The ability to see or visualise one's goals helps the idea sink into one's subconscious mind. Continued reinforcement is key.

It was also important for me to consider examples of what I had already achieved: overcoming obstacles associated with our move from Poland to South Africa, succeeding at school and on the sports field with a competitive spirit, being promoted in my career, and achieving academic success. There were also my other strong personal characteristics of focus, discipline, perseverance, and a firm belief in self.

I seemed to thrive on adversity, but I'm definitely not the only one in this world who can claim this. The history books are filled with examples. Two great role models that really made an impact in my life are Nelson Mandela – a universal symbol of freedom and reconciliation and the first black president of South Africa – and Lech Wałęsa – a labour activist who helped form and lead Poland's first independent trade union, Solidarity, and who was later president of the country.

I will prevail. I will cycle again, soon!

26

THE MINDSET TO LIVE WITH PAIN

One day, while listening to the lyrics of Pearl Jam's "Down", a line that spoke to how, when your symptoms for any kind of illness or predicament fade, you can throw the proverbial pills away, caused me to have an epiphany regarding how to absorb the pain I was experiencing.

After being involved in several boxing matches with pain, in the first weeks of my recovery, in which I was fighting its stranglehold on my body and mindset and its ultimate impact on my recovery, I came to a new-found realisation on how I was to deal with it in the future.

I realised that pain was no longer a physical phenomenon but rather a mental one. I had to call on every bit of my own strength of character, resilience, and will power to help me with what I was going to do. I also needed to draw on the overwhelming and positive support of my family, and particularly the influence of my grandfather, to make this shift of mindset.

From that day onwards, I would no longer be the victim of

pain. I would absorb it into my DNA; it would become part of my daily living. I would no longer show others how I was hurting. I would no longer talk about the pain, and personally I would no longer dwell on it.

This may sound like a utopic state to anyone going through hardship; but there is a catch. By shutting off the blows from the physical realm, your mind takes all of the knocks. It's a mind game.

At first, you don't even notice it, but with time, your mental resolve to continue on your chosen path can become very difficult or lonely, and this can cause you to slide into a black hole. This is a dangerous place to be. With mental fatigue, there can be no physical recovery, or even worse, your recovery can make a U-turn and land you back where you don't want to be. Depression and other mental or cognitive issues can occur.

You have to be mentally strong to achieve this. Your attitude, life philosophies, and inner strength need to be aligned, focused, unwavering, and strong – not only for today, but for every day.

Looking back at it now, my recovery was very much like any path that we take in our lives, where we have to get from point A to point B, with the journey being characterised by both peaks and troughs. The difference with the road to recovery or dealing with pain lies in the fact that the peaks, and especially the troughs, are more extreme. They are also more frequent; they don't occur every day or every couple of days but rather every minute or every second, even when you are undertaking a simple, remedial task. During these troughs, you have to search for hope and inspiration in order not to lose sight of your end goal.

Throughout my journey of recovery, from the first couple of weeks after coming out of a coma until today, my saving grace has been one simple thing … I always tried to not place focus on myself, my situation, my injuries, or my pain. That is a downward spiral which will suck you under quicker than a whirlpool.

In hindsight, it's astounding how easily I was able to turn off the realm of physical pain once I put my mind to it.

27

SOCIAL STIGMA

One never pays much attention to social stigma until you actually become the victim of such discrimination. Generally, it is the labelling of a person by members of the community on the grounds or characteristics of ethnicity, gender, religion, disease, status, race, and physical or medical conditions. These include external deformations such as scars or burns, physical appearance caused by anorexia or obesity, or addictions such as drug abuse or alcoholism.

People will generalise and stereotype others into boxes. It is deeply discrediting and calls into question the humanity of a person. Social stigma has social, psychological, and health consequences that, for example, lead to depression, low self-esteem, pity, and anger.

On my arrival in South Africa, I was exposed to social stigma to a small degree. We were a Polish family, new immigrants to South Africa, and we were based in Vanderbijlpark, a very Afrikaans-centred community. English was occasionally spoken but definitely not Polish! We were often called foreigners and many a time Waldek and I had to run or cycle for our lives to avoid getting into fights with the Afrikaans-speaking kids in the neighbourhood.

Now again, with the physical and mental injuries I had incurred in the accident, social stigma raised its ugly head. Those who had worked on me at the hospital didn't realise that the back of my head was damaged, or perhaps they didn't consider the damage to be serious in the bigger scheme of things. But after a couple of weeks of recovery, I realised that a huge scar had formed at the back of my head, one that no hair was brave enough to put its roots into.

I felt quite self-conscious about this, given the existing damages to my appearance. As such, I consulted a plastic surgeon and underwent an operation which resulted in 80 stitches in my head. I was bandaged like a mummy for a couple of days until I went for a check-up and the dressings were removed. This was in the latter part of the year, so the African heat made this quite uncomfortable.

I had to re-examine my self-esteem and confidence levels. I learnt to live with all of my scars, including the remaining C-shaped scar on the back of my head following the corrective plastic surgery, measuring 8 centimetres, as well as a 16-centimetre scar on the left side of my forehead and only half of which was concealed by my hair. I also have a tracheostomy scar on my throat, a 9-centimetre surgical scar on my left shoulder, a surgical scar of 6 centimetres on my left hand with deformity of the knuckles, a gastrostomy scar on my abdomen, and a linear scar measuring 16 centimetres, widening at one point to 4 centimetres, over my left knee.

Although I had witnessed the stigma associated with neurological trauma prior to the accident, I never really paid much attention to it. I always thought of social stigma as a third party, something outside of me. For instance, it was a general expectation that a person who suffered neurological trauma might not have a good memory.

It was only now, when I became the object of stigma, that I felt its ugliness and vulnerabilities. I adopted techniques to improve my memory which proved to be helpful. Nonetheless, deep inside of my heart I believed that my memory was still compromised.

All of this changed, one day, when I met my neurologist together with Waldek. The doctor asked me about the status of my memory and I gave him my truthful assessment, which was not very positive.

At that stage, my brother burst out laughing!

I asked him: "What is so funny?"

He replied: "What did you buy my wife for her birthday last year?" He was referring to Pauline's birthday the year before I'd had my accident.

I thought about it and could not recall, so I answered: "I cannot remember."

"Exactly, that is my point, you cannot remember!" echoed Waldek. He explained through his laughter that although he had reminded me about her birthday three times, I'd still forgotten about it and hadn't bought his wife a present.

This showed that, even before the accident, I'd forgotten about my sister-in-law's birthday in spite of many reminders. This gave me immense hope. This small example and realisation that my brother used helped me to bury a stigma that could've caused me much embarrassment and longer-term psychological difficulties down the line. It was also the catalyst to help my mental attitude and approach to my life during the road to recovery.

I was able to rise above the fears and inadequacies caused by social stigma and victimisation. I hope this will be an example to others who are experiencing the same feelings and occurrences in their lives.

28

DEFINING
THE UNEXPECTED

The accident was unexpected, the changes in my appearance were unexpected, and the changes to my body were unexpected. But once I learnt what had happened to me, I was able to gauge what was to be expected going forward.

In order to help me be better prepared for the road to recovery facing me, I was briefed about the typical consequences I could expect to occur following my traumatic brain injury. These included cognitive problems, such as headaches, difficulty thinking, memory issues, attention deficit, mood swings, language and communication difficulties, irritability, and frustration. What I didn't expect, found mind-blowing while at the same time bloody frustrating, was that, given the frontal-lobe damage, I lost my sense of smell and consequently my sense of taste. I also lost the ability to feel hunger.

I could eat everything and anything and it would taste like nothing. I became frustrated, to the point of murder, when someone asked me stupid questions like, "Was that nice?" or, "What would you like to eat?" I felt like each one was a reminder of my disability, which, at that time, I was prepared to ignore for a while.

Hunger is another gift that we all take for granted and which we rather view as a curse. However, once the gastrostomy tube was removed and I was no longer being fed by someone else, be that the nurses at the hospital or my mother at my house, people started to realise what a moody person I became after the accident. Most thought this was expected personality change given the brain injury I had suffered. Luckily, I once again had my two brothers who were sure to point out to me what a douchebag I had become. I did a lot of introspection, only to find out that my mood changes were immediate and coincided with the usual lunch and supper hours. It was at this time that I drew the two together and realised that my brain no longer registered the sensation of hunger. I went from Mister Nice Guy to Mister Moody And Irritable in a matter of seconds. I guess that it was the gastrostomy which "switched off" my body's need to monitor my hunger and inform the brain of it; maybe it was the damage to the frontal lobe, who knows. But to realise that I lost the sensation of feeling hungry, more basic in my view than smell and taste, was overwhelming to say the least.

I am happy to report that after a long time my sense of smell and thus taste have returned, and I'm able to experience hunger. It still baffles me how we take such simple things for granted, as if they're owed to us by our parents and the Creator.

29

RETURNING TO MY JOB AT THE BANK

A couple of months after the accident, the bank put me on their insurance cover for temporarily or permanently incapacitated persons, which meant that although I was receiving 75% of my salary, my job was no longer guaranteed. This was a hard blow to my confidence and an even bigger concern; would I be able to meet the standard of work they expected of me?

It took me a couple of months to be able to put pen to paper, and I had serious doubts about whether or not I'd ever be able to compete on the same level as my colleagues, some of whom held doctorates. This was really brought home to me when I attended the rehab sessions and couldn't even answer questions or repeat some of the most basic stories told to me.

I had to get my mind and body geared to returning to my bank duties. Thus far, my recovery and rehab sessions concentrated on my physical mishaps, memory deficiencies, and ability to communicate. My job as an operational risk manager within the bank's CIB division was an intellectually demanding one that involved identifying and analysing risks across the operational activities. The job also entailed coming up with strategies to mitigate these risks and to report them to senior management. It required an in-depth understanding of the bank's business processes and procedures, as well as of regulations governing operational risk. As part of my role, I had to engage numerous stakeholders of various levels of seniority across the different business units and group functions of the bank. I also had to liaise with the South African Reserve Bank, and other regulatory bodies, and present at various governance committees. It was important to be able to communicate clearly in writing as well as in speech. Researching complex topics, and reading and internalising large batches of material in order to develop solutions fit for the bank, was a standard part of the job.

In my work, I didn't have to liaise with external clients, but I interacted with internal clients throughout the day. This, to me, was more challenging than dealing with external clients, as my colleagues' opinions could quickly turn to gossip, which would certainly impact my future career prospects.

So, I started preparing myself to re-enter the corporate world. I had my laptop delivered to my ward, and in between the therapy and rehab sessions, I began typing and sending emails to all my family and friends. Later, I began reading material online related to my line of work, and I even studied a course in online trading. I didn't pass it, but that wasn't the main goal. I'd managed to get my mind working, remembering, and absorbing information. I'd also succeeded in preparing mentally to return to full-time employment.

I went back to work in December 2010, primarily on a light-duty basis. This meant doing reduced hours in a less-stressful working environment. However, it had the opposite effect on my mental attitude. I was stressed out and very nervous that I wouldn't cope with the demands of my job and that I'd be given my marching orders. It wasn't long, however, before my confidence returned, and within weeks, I was coping with my full job responsibilities on a full-time basis.

Although that was a blessing, it also came with additional stress. Being office-bound implies sitting quite a bit, either at your desk or in meeting rooms. After a couple of days, my back would seize up. I'd be sitting at my desk, trying to type something, or to be mentally present and to contribute to the meeting, while it felt like someone was riding a tank over my upper back, all the time firing heavy guns at and planting mines in the muscles around and below my shoulder blades. Given the pain, every second week I had to see a massage therapist who would apply her or his magic to my back for 30 minutes. This continues to be the case today. Every other week, I see a chiropractor who applies her or his science to my back for an additional half an hour. These treatments provide me with temporary relief; sometimes, when I feel particularly down, I fear that only death will provide me with total relief. Then I cling to those Pearl Jam lyrics that remind me not to let the light escape from me, or to allow the darkness to swallow me, and I get up regardless of where I am, regardless of who is in the meeting, and stretch, as best I can, to alleviate some degree of this nightmarish pain.

I wish I could say that my back is the only disability that bothers me at work, but like in every good horror movie, there's more. The blind spot in my right eye has a certain brightness around its edges, or perhaps a certain magnification of light is a better explanation of it. In darker spaces, that doesn't bother me too much, but when I have to sit staring at a computer screen for a while, the magnification of the light becomes blinding, for which there are only two solutions. Either step away or look away to allow the eye time to readjust or, when under time pressure, cover the eye with the right hand while typing with the left. The only problem with the latter solution is that my left hand was also quite damaged in the accident. So, although I can type with it, I can't ever be as proficient with it as I am with my right hand.

Nonetheless, I managed to deal with these disabilities, and continue to do so today. Within a very short space of time, and certainly with the invaluable help and support of my superiors, Howard Baxter, Paul Rew, and Richard Pantcheff, I was eventually promoted to an even more senior position, as a director of a division within Standard Bank.

This promotion came a little less than a year after my accident. I was 31 years of age and now Group Head of Operational Risk Framework and Methodologies, which entailed the design of and participation in the implementation of a group-wide operational risk framework.

A little later, I accepted a post with another bank, Barclays (now Absa Bank). The move to Absa also came with added responsibilities.

30

BACK ON
THE BIKE

I have already mentioned that there was one goal driving me all the time: to cycle again. It became an all-consuming objective of mine, a burning desire, and it is one of the factors that got me to where I am today.

My initial goal was to compete in an easier race, the 94.7 Cycle Challenge sponsored by financial-services company Momentum. This would be one of the stepping stones for me to face my ultimate test, The Epic, a marathon eight-day cycle race around the Western Cape winelands. My family, the doctors, and the nursing staff thought I was mad.

On the day I purchased my new bicycle, I got dressed in my riding gear, held the bicycle, and smiled and smiled. I think it was the first time that I'd smiled since the accident and some three or four months since coming out of the coma. It was one of the happiest days of my life. With my new bicycle in full view of my bed and chair, I could see my dream, I could touch my dream. I needed to see it every day. I was getting close, very close!

And my family saw it every day, and at times shook their heads. But it was my dream and no one was going to steal my dream. Many people have given up on their dreams based on what others have said to them. I've realised that one shouldn't belittle anyone's dream; for some, that is all they have. There is a lovely inspirational quote by Japanese manga artist Hiro Mashima that reads: "You have three choices in life, *give in, give up,* or *give it your all.*"

The first time I got onto my new bicycle, I was very nervous and realised, to my dismay, how weak I really was. My legs just could not move, particularly my right leg where I'd had the problem with the calcification around the knee. Waldek actually had to assist me and physically move my legs to get the momentum going. Slowly, as the months passed, my physical condition began to improve. I didn't have confidence in my riding ability at that stage, so I would only venture out when Waldek and Adrian joined me for a training ride. I was still suffering badly with my back and vision. Given my blind spot, I needed someone to cycle with me and to shout out warnings.

My immediate aim was to ride the 94.7 Cycle Challenge with a slower group of riders. One way to do this was to cycle for a charity. Ride for a Purpose allows cyclists to create awareness around and raise funds for a cause or charity close to their hearts. But at that stage, I wasn't too interested in the philanthropic aspect of the ride. It may sound a bit selfish, but my personal goal was to not fall off the bicycle and to complete the race, no matter how long it would take me.

And so, just over six months after the accident, I was back in the saddle, with a good dose of fear, uncertainty, and doubt, competing in the 94.7. Waldek and my friend Greg Judin escorted me as protection against road hazards and other riders. We completed the race successfully without any incidents.

I know this achievement was hailed and recognised by my family, friends, and work colleagues as a significant victory, but for me it felt as if I'd won Gold at the Olympics. Six months earlier, I was in a coma fighting for my life; five months earlier,

I couldn't walk; four months earlier, I couldn't fully rotate the peddle. To me, this was a huge personal triumph and a major morale booster.

The success of my cycling achievement and the confidence I gained from being on the road also helped me to get back behind the steering wheel and drive my car again. This milestone I achieved in little less than a year after the accident.

But I wasn't finished or fully content with my achievements to date. I could not sit back and relax. I had to continue to push myself. The bigger test was still to come: The Epic.

31

THE CAPE EPIC

The Epic, which takes place every year but never follows the exact same course, has been deemed *hors catégorie* (French for "beyond categorisation") by the Union Cycliste Internationale, the world governing body for sports cycling. It is ridden over eight days, consisting of a prologue and seven stages. The 2013 race covered 706 kilometres and was, as it is in any other year, an extremely enduring race through the mountainous area of the Cape Winelands. The course included 15 950 metres of vertical gain, equivalent to nearly twice the height of Mount Everest.

The idea to do The Epic came in the form of an angelic voice that blew with the wind into my ear over my titanium shoulder. In retrospect ... I am still unsure whether I should consider Waldek's voice to be angelic; perhaps the opposite is true.

The Epic attracts elite, professional mountain bikers from around the world who compete in teams of two. To qualify for a finish, teams have to stay together for the duration of the race, meaning they cannot be more than two minutes apart at any time while riding. The race is also open to amateurs, who enter a lottery in order to gain an entry. A total of 650 teams took part in 2013.

This wasn't the first time that Waldek and I had considered The Epic; in fact, we actually paid for our entry into the 2010 Epic, and started the early preparation for it. This would've been our biggest challenge on the mountain bike at that stage of our lives, and it put firecrackers, also known as ball-breaking and utter fear, in our arses. However, Pauline fell pregnant and, before we knew it, was scheduled to welcome their son, Alexander, to the world during the time that we would've been away. After multiple, well-reasoned, totally objective but failed attempts at explaining to Pauline that the father does not actually need to be present during the birth of his second child, we graciously agreed to sell our 2010 Epic entries and remain put in Johannesburg ... not cycling. After all, Pauline was the mother of my god-daughter, the lovely and talented Carmen, so I had already developed a soft side for children.

Thus, undertaking the 2013 Epic put me, mentally, physically, and in my heart, at the same point I was at in 2009, prior to my accident. That was quite an achievement, but if I could actually undertake The Epic, finish it, and even ride well, it would be proof to me that I was more capable or stronger now than I was prior to the accident.

Entering the 2013 Epic put those firecrackers back under our arses. However, this time my fear was multiplied with every broken bone I'd sustained and with the realisation that a wheelchair or the loss of limb was never as far away as I'd thought it was in the past.

In addition to the nervousness that The Epic induces, the commitment to do it, as well as the training required to prepare for it, plants nuclear bombs under the base of any solid relationship. Our training spanned six months: six days a week, with Mondays as rest days but no more off days whatsoever in between aside from those owing to childbirth which, luckily this time, there was none of.

As with any training programme, we were eased into it before it got really nasty and before it put major strain on our bodies and relationships. At the beginning, peak weeks involved 16 hours of training; this spiked to 22 hours in the last couple of months. Cycling 22 hours in a week implied riding 2 hours a day from Tuesday to Friday, which left 14 hours for the weekend. This meant waking up at 3.30 am so that we could cycle before the roads got too busy and dangerous during weekdays. It also meant that in order to get 8 hours of sleep we had to be in bed and asleep by 20.30 pm; say bye-bye to your relationship or the idea of getting lucky! During weekends, we had to cycle 7 hours a day, which is already as long as a normal working day less a lunch hour. However, at this point in the training, we were so tired of cycling the same route that we ended up driving to cycle somewhere else, giving us a 9-hour day.

Despite the long, torturous hours, mountain biking and getting in touch with nature, especially in the South African spring and summer, was breathtakingly beautiful. However, the devil always lurks in beauty. The flashing lights, caused by contrasting light and shadow when cycling through a grove of trees, for example, made me fear the onset of an epileptic fit. My fear of seizures stemmed from the fact that I was made aware of the risk of post-traumatic epilepsy due to the focal nature of my brain injury and penetration of the brain by bone in the left frontal area. This was compounded by the fact that I was on a bicycle, travelling relatively fast through, over, or past nature's minefields disguised as trees, rocks, river crossings, and steep downhills.

A successful week, especially those with more than 18 hours of cycling, implied riding the bike when the sun was shining, when it was pissing like dogs and bitterly cold, when I was feeling strong, when I was too weak to open my eyes, when I was happy, when I was in the doldrums not seeing the light, when my back was paralysed stiff from pain and my right knee ached with every peddle rotation, when I was afraid of being hit by a car again but chose to put my trust in God, and when I felt that I'd bitten off too much and was now choking on my commitment but knew that the pain of giving up and of choosing a version of me that I was unwilling to accept was not an option given the money and time we'd spent.

Fearing that my back would give in, we added Pilates to our training. We attended two classes per week and it yielded greater value than what money could buy. Don't get me wrong, it wasn't the answer to everything that is wrong with this world, and my back still took a beating during The Epic and in the training leading up to it. I do however believe that without the Pilates training I would not have been able to complete the race.

After the training was over and our bikes were serviced and our bags packed, we flew to Cape Town with excitement and all of our spoken and unspoken doubts and fears in our pockets, ready to compete in the race.

The race starts off with a prologue that is short but brutal. Everyone wants to do their best on the first day in order to improve their seeding and start batch for the next day, which ultimately has a knock-on effect for seeding on the days to follow. Waldek started the prologue like a machine on steroids. They say when a person trains at altitude they perform better at sea level – that was certainly true for Waldek but completely the opposite for me. The prologue is also characterised by steep hills, which Waldek simply ignored but which were punching me in the face. After a while I however managed to get things under control and got my legs back. While climbing one hill, I became quite confident that we would get a good placing by the end of the stage. Just then, as we reached the top of the hill and were about to start a proper descent, I changed a gear, put my foot down, and snapped the chain! Waldek and I were off the bikes, swearing and bitching at one another while trying to fix the problem at hand. Having a broken chain is always a major issue on a normal stage, which is about 90 kilometres long, but on a prologue, which is only 20-odd kilometres long, it is a complete disaster. We managed to fix the chain and rushed to try make up the lost time, which we were unable to do.

Over the next couple of days, we aimed to improve our seeding and start batch. By stage three, on day four, we managed to get ourselves into the start batch we believed we belonged in, but by then we already knew that we'd lost too much time in order to meet our unofficial goal of a top-100 finish.

Cycling The Epic made me reach my limit each and every day. My fears were magnified during stage four when, absolutely flying on a fairly technical section, we passed one of the top, leading pro ladies' teams and saw that they were lying in the dirt, one of the riders holding her arm as though it was broken. That put the brakes on in my heart and I slowed down somewhat during the more technical sections. Luckily, I had Waldek, who cursed me and called me names until I put my fear and/or common sense aside and pushed on. I do have to say that without my brother there and by my side outside of The Epic, I would perhaps never have pushed myself as hard as I did, so perhaps an insult or two is just what the doctor ordered.

On another day, the mechanics told us that the rocker links – a part of the bike that connects the rear shock to the frame – on both of our bikes were cracked and that there were no spares to fix the problem. We rode three or four stages fearing that when we were flying from the steepest, rockiest hill imaginable, a rocker would come apart and one of our bikes would collapse, leaving the rider to kiss the rocks with his broken teeth. At this stage, my back, although massaged daily, was already at its limit. I rode in fear every day and went to bed in pain, hoping I could get up the next morning without something giving way.

Usually, the field of riders would split up some in the middle of the stage and we would find ourselves riding alone for a while. Slowing down was out of the question, therefore we would just keep going to ensure that we had a good finish for the day and climbed up the general classification. It was at times like these that we would take turns to swap the lead with each other in order to preserve our energy. The route was always clearly marked, so there was little to no risk that we would stray off course and lose time; that is, until I came to the front. I don't know how many times I took the lead and after cycling like a complete champ for a couple of kilometres turned in the direction opposite to what was indicated. The blind spot in my right eye was really playing on my nerves after a while. Luckily, I always heard the stern voice of Waldek, the eagle eye, very impolitely requesting in very colourful language that a U-turn be performed immediately!

On the eighth day of the race, and three years after the accident, Waldek and I, in an upbeat spirit of reconciliation, held one of each other's hands up in the air as we crossed the finish line for the last stage of the 2013 Cape Epic.

Although I'd had my fears and had been scared to death that my back might've given way and that I may have landed up in a wheelchair again, or that I may have fallen and ruined my left shoulder or my previously cracked skull, we had proceeded onwards throughout the race. We didn't finish in the top 100 but rather were placed 115th, within the top 15% of all finishers, including the professional teams!

32

AFTER
THE CAPE EPIC

I was sick and tired of training. I wanted to go back to the idea of cycling just for the pure love of it, which accounts for some of my greatest cycling moments. In truth, The Epic took so much out of me, both mentally and physically, that I needed some downtime. One year, a bunch of mates organised a cycling tour in Europe and invited Waldek and me. This was idyllic, cycling with mates up some of the most magical climbs of the Tour de France, getting to a small town, buying some baguettes, cheese, and prosciutto, and having a snack while sitting on the steps of a church.

On this specific tour, Waldek and I, against our instincts, decided to rent bicycles overseas as opposed to flying our bikes over. On the positive side, it made the trip easier, as we didn't have to drag huge bike bags with us; we didn't have to worry about some careless idiot at the airport throwing the bike bags from one place to another; and we didn't have to worry that our bikes wouldn't arrive at the next point. What we *did* have to worry about, and only found out to our surprise while cycling, was that, unlike our bikes in South Africa on which the front brake lever was on the left-hand side of the handlebar, these rented bikes had the brake lever on the right. This might not seem like a train smash, but when you're thundering down the Col du Télégraphe and you're taking a corner, pressing the incorrect lever instinctively could land you on the road with oncoming traffic, or have you tumbling over the concrete road barriers to undertake a small degree of sky-diving before meeting with the hard terrain of the mountain – which I almost did on this trip; *man, that was close!*

To add to this, the rim of a wheel erodes over time through braking, which decreases the rim's thickness, and when you're flying down the Col du Tourmalet and braking a lot, the rim becomes warmer. As the rim heats up, the eight-bar of air in the tire expands, subsequently putting more pressure on the thinner side of the rim. I learnt this while hurtling down this magnificent mountain pass: while I was travelling on a straight part of the downhill, the rear wheel exploded, causing it to jam. I have no idea how I kept my cool, but somehow I managed to stop the bike without an incident.

Although I experienced these near-fatal events, tours such as these have stuck as my firm-favourite rides; being able to cycle up some of those cols and seeing how the weather and vegetation changes, from sunny with grass and cows to bitterly cold with a dash of frozen snow on the side. This tour was an amazing experience I never thought I'd experience. I remain thankful for being given another opportunity at life and feel blessed that I was able to partake in it regardless of my fear of my known issues today and the issues that may manifest tomorrow.

PART V

MY LIFE SINCE
THE ACCIDENT

33

ERNA, THE LOVE
OF MY LIFE

It was early December 2011; Christmas was fast approaching. The mood in the country was already very festive. Soon thousands of people and their families would be taking their annual leave and heading to holiday destinations all over South Africa or even further abroad.

It was about a year since I'd returned to work after the accident. In another team complementing my own in the risk-management division at the bank, I noticed this lovely brunette.

I learnt that her name was Erna Terblanche but was warned that she was in a relationship, so it was hands-off. I was single at the time, having parted with my girlfriend, Alexandra, some months earlier. On reflection, I must thank Alexandra and her family for all the support and love they showered on me, especially in those dark days during my recovery and rehabilitation. She constantly visited me while I was in a coma and afterwards, at great personal sacrifice to herself and her daughter.

Erna, who hailed from the Eastern Cape, where her brother and parents lived, had attended North-West University in Potchefstroom, where she got her degree, a BCom Honours in Risk Management.

Erna had joined the bank's graduate-development programme in 2008, which implied spending six months undergoing intensive training, with short-term, select strategic job rotations within different segments of the bank. Thereafter, she got a more permanent job placement in her area of interest, the risk-management division.

Fate would have it that we both ended up working on the same floor and were seated fairly close to each other. It was very convenient for me to find time and excuses to chat to Erna while we were at the office.

That December, Erna had just broken off a romantic relationship, so the coast was clear for me to chat to and get to know her. Following the accident, and my break-up, I was far more withdrawn, less confident and, in all honesty, hadn't really been chasing women.

Some people think I've changed somewhat since the accident and being in a coma. Yes, I do think I've changed, but I also believe that people over-dramatise this. I don't believe that you just wake up a totally changed man overnight. I try my best to appreciate things each and every day regardless of how mundane they may seem. Some days I succeed, some days I fail. I am not as impatient as before but, at the same time, I am no longer willing to put my life on the back seat to meet some idea of future happiness. Happiness is right here with all of us; it is in the mundane.

For the next couple of months, I was able to spend more time at the office talking to Erna and getting to understand her a lot better. Erna is a very beautiful person with many wonderful characteristics, certainly someone I love to be around. She is humble, kind, caring, and yet able to hold her head and opinion high where need be. Erna has a remarkable sense of humour … which is great, as she actually finds my quirky jokes funny. Her one priority, at least in my view, is to ensure that others are happy. This, I thought, would no doubt ensure that Erna would be a loving and caring mother and wife one day.

It was on Valentine's Day in 2012 that I plucked up the courage and formally invited Erna for dinner and, as they say in the classics, the rest is history. Our romance sparked and ignited, and within a year, Erna moved in with me. At that stage, I owned a house in a secure complex in Edenvale, an eastern suburb of greater Johannesburg.

We had many common interests, including running and travelling, and later Erna started cycling as well. Erna was the adventurous type and also loved horses. That was her form of escapism whereas for me it was cycling. Our interests gave each of us a sense of freedom and allowed us to escape from the rat race in the concrete jungle. Although I have, on the odd occasion, ridden horses with Erna, which I must confess I really enjoyed, I needed to realistically consider the consequences should I ever fall off. The probability of which was astronomical, given my lack of horse-riding skills. The repercussions, given my medical history, the titanium plates in my face, head, and shoulder, as well as my injured back and my knee issues, could be devastating. Hence, I am not as in love with horse-riding as I am with cycling ... where I still somehow believe my survival chances are greater. Man logic.

I realised that I really wanted to build my life and my future with this fabulous person.

34

THE PENDULUM

One of the ways to win a girl over is to be liked by her parents. Meeting and getting to know your partner's parents can be quite intimidating for any dating couple.

Before we were married, we went away for Easter weekend with Erna's parents to Hogsback, a magical world in the Amathole Mountains of the Eastern Cape, surrounded by indigenous Afromontane forests that are hundreds of years old. It's a wonderful place to get away from the rush of city life, to be immersed in picturesque surroundings, to enjoy activities such as hiking and mountain biking, and, above all, to relax in the silence and tranquillity.

We rented two lovely cabins at The Edge Mountain Retreat, which was built right on the verge of a deep ravine and had the best views of the mountains and the valley.

We however ended up being stuck inside the cabins for the whole weekend owing to the severe rain and fog, unseasonable for that time of the year. The blanket of fog was so thick that we couldn't even see the view for which the resort is known. Due to mud slides, the road down the mountain was impassable by car. To add to this, it was freezing, and we were naïve in having not packed much warm clothing. Given that the road was unusable, we were unable to get to the shops to buy more clothes. We however made the best of our circumstances. We spent great quality time together with Erna's parents just by sitting near the fireplace, playing card games, and drinking sherry. It was certainly a good way for all of us to get to know each other.

It was just one of those times when things are not under your control, when nature deals you a certain hand. In this case, I needed to play the cards I was dealt and just go with the flow. There is always a plan B in life.

By the latter part of 2014, after dating for two years, our relationship grew stronger and I felt that Erna started to become a bit anxious as to when or whether I would pop the question. We planned a trip to romantic Capri, but I didn't want my proposal to be such an MTV cliché. Capri is a heavenly island in the Tyrrhenian Sea off the coast of Naples in Italy. One day, we decided to charter a boat which took us all around the island to see the caves and wonderful snorkelling spots. These were so stunning that we wanted to see more of them. So, the next day, wanting to avoid the exorbitant tourist prices and being crammed into a chartered boat like a bunch of sardines with other tourists, we came up with a simple solution: rent our own boat and navigate it ourselves. Neither of us had any experience with boats, but we were willing to try it. We didn't know what to expect, but it was surely bound to be fun.

Our "bound-to-be-fun" sea voyage quickly turned unpleasant as the sea became extremely choppy and rough. I was doing my best to steer the boat to avoid the high waves, but Erna became extremely seasick, hanging over the side of the boat for half of the voyage. This is where I found myself in a pendulum. On the one side, I truly felt concerned for Erna's well-being and was a bit fearful that our boat might capsize and we would drown. However, as the pendulum swung from left to right, I felt complete bliss. There I was, commanding my boat through the stormy weather, whereas, just a couple of years ago, I was bound within a radius of about 90 kilometres around Edenvale, unable to leave as I felt paralysed and trapped by my back pain.

Erna and I have had quite a few amazing and adventurous trips together. But most of the stories that we all hear from other people about their lives are their Facebook moments. You know, only those specific highlights in our lives that we choose to share with family and friends on social media. People don't typically post the reverse side of the pendulum for others to see, for example: "Girlfriend, who thinks Boyfriend will propose to her on idyllic island but does not, is now puking from a boat while Boyfriend is chasing Free Willy." This is the side of the pendulum where we need to find our happiness; not only in the fearful or exciting times, but also in the everyday and sometimes-mundane moments such as when we are washing dishes, hanging the laundry out to dry, or changing a child's nappy for the sixth time during a night in which you haven't slept a wink.

35

HIGH TEA IN
THE PALACE

Erna and I had now been courting for over two and a half years, and I sensed that she was well past the "a-bit-anxious" stage, so I needed to move quickly … but if you want the proposal to be a unique surprise, then you also need to do a lot of planning and perhaps take a person or two into your confidence.

Being a somewhat old-fashioned guy, I first needed to ask Erna's parents for their permission to marry her. I felt that this was the right thing to do, especially for their only daughter. The opportunity presented itself when Erna's parents, Otto and Ilse Terblanche, were visiting us in Johannesburg and accompanied us for a few days to Sun City Resort, a famous holiday destination, established in 1979 by Sol Kerzner, some two hours' drive from Johannesburg.

At Sun City, however, I struggled to find the appropriate time to speak to Erna's parents. Erna and her mom were in each other's company all the time. I needed to find a way to speak to them without Erna knowing.

There are various hotels and places of accommodation within Sun City Resort, but The Palace of the Lost City is the flagship five-star hotel. Every detail of The Palace has been carefully considered to ensconce guests in opulent comfort. Only the very wealthy stay at this hotel, with access and security for its patrons being strictly controlled. Visitors from the rest of the resort are not permitted onto The Palace premises.

I deemed this an appropriate place to ask for Erna's parents' permission, even if I would only propose to Erna at a later stage. I always take one of my bicycles with me on holiday, so I cycled to The Palace on my mountain bike, and after an extended negotiation with the security staff, I eventually got to meet the hotel manager, who agreed to accommodate me. I told him we were guests at the Vacation Club resort and that I wanted to ask my girlfriend's parents for their blessing to marry their daughter, and would appreciate it if I could do this in the wonderful ambience and opulence of The Palace.

I set it up that we would have high tea there the following day. Obviously, I didn't divulge my undercover mountain-biking expedition to my audience, so when I suggested to Erna and her parents that we go to The Palace for high tea, they said, "You'll never get in."

I tried to concoct a plan to ensure that I would be alone with Erna's parents first before Erna arrived, but for the life of me I didn't know how I could sell such an absurd scheme to the ladies. I therefore came up with something else: Erna's dad and I would go up to The Palace first to see if we could get in; if we were lucky, we'd call Erna and her mom to join us. This way, they wouldn't be embarrassed if we got thrown out.

Erna's dad is a professor of history, so our plan was to introduce him as a visiting professor from Holland; I would be a photographer from Europe who wanted to investigate the suitability of The Palace as a possible future conference venue.

Given that Erna's dad didn't know I'd previously arranged access to The Palace and its restaurant, he was quite surprised at how easily we got in, and we remained incognito. It was there that I asked his permission to marry his daughter and was much relieved when he immediately agreed. We decided to keep the matter between us to ensure that Erna didn't find out about my intentions.

I then arranged for The Palace's courtesy car to go and fetch Erna and her mom and for them to join us for a remarkable high tea. They were in disbelief that we'd actually pulled it off. Otto and I stuck to our story and acted out our parts, of photographer and visiting professor, when the waitrons served us or came near the table.

I was obviously unable to get Erna's mom's blessing, and this has come back to bite me, as Ilse has never forgiven me and Otto for withholding this information from her. But, given the circumstances, it was the best that I could've done.

Back in Johannesburg, and given that I'd gotten Erna's father's blessing, timing was against me. I now had to act fast and propose to Erna before the cat got out of the bag.

But, as stated earlier, great ideas take time to execute.

We often visited our friends Paulo and Michelle da Camara in Waterfall Estate, an area in the north of Johannesburg. We both liked the setup in and around this estate, which had the sense of freedom and space of a nature reserve within the confines of a city. In addition to the setting, the security, and the fact that it was a little closer to our work, were great drawcards.

I ended up buying a plot in the estate and we planned to build our dream house there. At this stage, the architectural plans were finalised, and we had chosen the builder, who was meant to be on site. But this builder, like any other, was already running late with the project and wasting our money.

On Saturday, 8 November 2014, about a month after I had asked for Erna's hand, I mentioned to her that we had to go investigate and resolve a problem at our building site: the builder had placed a portable toilet there before getting clearance to start the building process, and we would therefore be liable for a steep fine from the estate management. I pretended to be angry about this, and it certainly revved up Erna.

We were living in Edenvale at that time, about 30 minutes' drive from our plot, and when we arrived at the site that morning, sure enough, there was a large tent in the middle of the stand. I muttered in amazement that the portable toilet was probably inside the tent. I had hardly said these words when Erna was off ... marching to the tent, closely followed by me.

Erna opened the flap, and before her were cushions neatly spread out on a blanket, with a picnic laid out and champagne and glasses set up on a table. It was then, as I entered the tent, that I dropped onto one knee and asked the vital question, "Erna, will you marry me?"

Her reaction was priceless. She was taken by complete surprise. The answer, you can guess, was ... a tearful ... "Yes" ...

It made my day to see Erna so happy. After the second glass of champagne, we phoned our parents and close family members to tell them our exciting news.

Paulo, who stayed at the estate, had helped to organise the props and the right theme, for which I remain eternally thankful.

I guess you are wondering about the ring?

Paulo's brother-in-law, a jeweller, designed it to my specifications, helping me with the details and providing me with links and tips to get the right measurement. The big stone represented my love for Erna, and the little stones were symbolic of all the hard work that we had done and would need to do to make our relationship and marriage work and to foster and deepen our love for each other every day. Marriage is a partnership, in which both individuals need to commit to each other, not for a day but for a lifetime.

It took 14 months to build our home. The house is a double storey, a contemporary modern home, unassuming from the street, with its beauty being centred on the garden.

36

A LITTLE TASTE
OF MY HERITAGE

We set our wedding date for mid-December 2015, which was when we normally took our annual leave and which would fit in well with my proposed honeymoon destination.

We invited our Polish family, hoping some could attend, but unfortunately, it wasn't possible for most of them to come given the costs involved. So, I did the next best thing: I decided to take my fiancée to Poland, to introduce her to the family and to give her a little taste of my heritage.

Unfortunately, my beloved grandfather had passed away about two years earlier. He was 94 years of age, so his was a great innings to say the least.

Our trip to Poland took place in August 2015. My cousins organised a party for us which ended up almost being the equivalent of a full-on wedding reception. Erna was blown away by my Polish family's hospitality and warmth and the amount of effort they made to make the occasion so special for us. The family came together from all over the country to unite and to celebrate with us. The festivities were marked by speeches, a band that played traditional Polish music, and lots of dancing.

The family put together a wonderful spread, a buffet that was laid out on long tables and which consisted of traditional Polish dishes from both the north and the south of the country. I really missed a lot of those dishes and they certainly brought back fond memories of my youth in Poland, particularly of school holidays on my grandparents' farm. For Erna, it was an opportunity to sample the delicacies.

I also hinted to Erna that she'd better get hold of some of the recipes so we could enjoy these dishes back in South Africa. Erna can make a wonderful Polish tomato soup. I'm sure that with time she'll experiment with other Polish dishes.

My cousins clubbed their money together to hire a limousine which took us as well as my cousins all over town for a pre-wedding after-party.

Back in South Africa, the wedding plans were gathering momentum. I had always wanted to get married on a wine farm. There are plenty of wonderful spots scattered all around Cape Town and surrounds. Erna often visited and spent many family holidays with her grandparents in Paarl, about 40 minutes' drive from Cape Town. She had a soft spot for this location and wanted to get married there. We visited the area a few months before we set the wedding date and found a lovely farm called Diamant Estate, so goal number one, of finding the perfect venue, had been achieved.

As part of our wedding-planning activities, we needed to meet with and talk to the pastor, a personal friend of Erna's parents, as he had agreed to marry us. The idea was to finalise the arrangements with him and to receive his pre-marital couples' counselling.

We therefore went to Nelson Mandela Bay (previously known as Port Elizabeth) for a weekend to visit Erna's parents and to see the pastor. We arranged to meet with him at his house at 2 pm on a particular afternoon, and seeing that I had plenty of time to kill before our meeting, I decided to go for a quick mountain-bike ride in a nearby nature reserve in Nelson Mandela Bay that was being advertised as a prime cycling venue.

I ended up getting so lost that I completely missed the meeting with the pastor. Erna met with him alone for pre-marital counselling, and she single-handedly had to finalise our wedding plans. When I finally did arrive at Erna's parents' house, I hung my head low as I realised that my earlier endeavours to win Erna's parents over may have been somewhat compromised … and then there was my wife to deal with too.

On my wedding day, when the pastor arrived and greeted me, he laughed and remarked, "So happy to see you are not on your bicycle and were able to make this appointment!"

37

BELLS CHIME IN THE VINEYARDS

Our wedding took place on Wednesday, 16 December 2015, which was a public holiday in South Africa (the Day of Reconciliation) at Diamant Estate, set amidst the backdrop of the Paarl Mountain, beautiful views, manicured lawns, vineyards, and oak trees.

On the morning of the wedding, we woke up to overcast conditions and rain. Fortunately, the sun soon came out and it ended up being a beautiful day.

Erna had four bridesmaids, and I had five groomsmen. These included Waldek, Adrian, and three friends from school: Paulo, Heinrich, and Sacha.

Sacha and I have been friends since my early school days after arriving in South Africa. We matriculated together. Paulo was initially Waldek's friend from university, but later, our friendship deepened when we shared accommodation in Johannesburg. Our acquaintance went back some 15 years. Heinrich was Waldek's classmate, and similarly to Paulo, I got to know him a lot better when we shared accommodation after I moved from Vanderbijlpark to Johannesburg to start my working career. I had very little money at that stage of my life, and I also had no idea of where I could live in Johannesburg that would be secure, and Heinrich allowed me to stay with him until I could earn my first couple of salaries and was on my feet.

The wedding ceremony was held in an intimate stone building which had been converted into a chapel from an old wine cellar dating from the 1700s. We had just under 100 guests. I was privileged that Adam, my cousin from my dad's side, had made the trip from Poland to attend our wedding. It was a real joy to spend some time with him before the function. The wedding started at 4 pm and the celebrations continued until 4 am the next morning. Rumours are that I was one of the last men standing!

38

CLEAR-BLUE WATERS IN THE SEYCHELLES

Erna and I headed off for our honeymoon two days after our wedding. We went to a resort on Sainte Anne Island in the Seychelles. Sainte Anne is a private island that is surrounded by one of the largest marine parks in the Indian Ocean. We spent lazy days on pristine beaches punctuated by granite rocks and fringed by palm trees. When we were in need of more excitement, we went snorkelling at the coral reefs close to the island. The water was clear-blue and invitingly warm to swim in.

Late one afternoon, we went for a swim. The water was so pleasant that I decided to stay in long after my wife got out to go lay down on a sun lounger on the beach. While Erna was reading a book, I just sat in the shallow water, enjoying an ice-cold beer and the magnificent view in front of me. Turquoise-blue water stretched out endlessly to meet the disappearing sun on the horizon. Every now and then, I was joined by a school of small fish that swarmed around me. At one stage, Erna called out, "Look to your left!" and I managed to turn just in time to see a manta ray disappearing into the gently lapping waves. Watching the sunset in this idyllic moment led me to reflect on my accident.

Could it really only have been five years since I'd woken from a coma, with barely any chance of surviving, and with severe head and other injuries to my body that required extensive rehabilitation? Could it really only have been five years since I'd managed to battle and overcome the tremendous pain and self-doubt I had faced every day while recovering, learning to speak and walk again, and learning to integrate into society again? I realised in that moment the importance of embracing life not only in the great moments, such as this one, when I found myself watching the sunset amidst a paradise-like setting on our honeymoon, but also in the bad moments, when you may feel defeated by the curveballs thrown at you in life, as well as in the mundane, everyday moments in between.

Since my accident in April 2010, I have been resolved to be an optimistic person, someone who remains upbeat and humorous, with a positive perspective on life. Good and bad exists in every situation; you have a choice as to what you'll focus on. Every day when I wake up, I make a point of looking at the X-rays of my broken skull, and I remind myself that no matter what happens that day, I am alive and I have a lot to be thankful for. I set out to make the most of that day, to live my life to the fullest, as no one knows when it will be their last moment.

39

PAYING IT FORWARD

I have always believed that one should find a person who has suffered more than you and let him or her be your inspiration. I wanted to help and share my story with people – to give them hope.

The opportunity presented itself to me one day when Waldek mentioned Headway Gauteng, an NPO that his business, an accounting and auditing company, was doing work for. Headway offers a variety of therapeutic and social support programmes to survivors of acquired brain injuries, as well as support services to survivors' families and caregivers.

The vast majority of Headway's members have sustained a TBI as a result of motor-vehicle accidents, falls, sporting injuries, or medical conditions such as strokes, tumours, or illnesses such as meningitis. Headway also offers support to their members, some of whom have no ability to pay their medical bills.

These were once people like me who lived a full life up until the time of their injury, which then caused changes to their physical, cognitive, emotional, and/or social well-being. Through this NPO and its programmes, survivors and their families get practical advice, a better understanding about the brain injury the survivor has sustained, and some insight into the prognosis. At the same time, Headway helps the survivor's family to learn how they can make a meaningful contribution to the recovery of their loved one.

To achieve these objectives, the organisation has formed what is known as the Headway Friendship Circle and offers regular meetings. It is through sharing, caring, and being with others that a survivor's family feels less alone and is more able to cope. I sometimes attend and speak at this forum, to give hope and support to the survivors, to encourage their families, to answer any questions they have, or to discuss any issues they are struggling with.

Today, I try to be a role model to many people, especially those with brain injuries and those fighting social stigma. In all humbleness, I reiterate that I am not a perfect man and I do not profess to have all the answers. However, what I do share with these survivors is something that we have in common: I was once like them, emerging from a coma, tied to a bed, locked in my body, and fighting for survival. And I achieved it. I went through the pain, the social stigma, the rehab, and the mind games, to get to where I am today. If I could do it, then so can they.

Incidentally, while visiting some of the members at Headway, I asked about their experiences with speech therapy. Interestingly enough, they told me that during their hospital stay, prior to arriving at Headway, they too had received similar therapy to what I'd been subjected to.

It is my personal belief, having also encountered this situation first-hand, that medical practitioners and people in general tend to discount that a person who does not formulate a sentence or remember a word, might still be functional in their own mind. These survivors, depending on the extent of their injuries, will be able to follow a story or have an understanding of a word or concept, but for a myriad of reasons, they are trapped in their mind and there is a breakdown or slowness in the flow of communication (if there is any at all) to the recipient. Rather than all patients being subjected to a unilateral programme, each one should be given rehabilitation tasks unique to that person's current condition. Think of the case of Stephen Hawking here – were it not for the development of technology, 35 years ago, that allowed him to voice his thoughts, we would never have heard his brilliant mind.

40

THE FINANCIAL IMPACT ON TBI SURVIVORS

There is one thing that we tend to discount when someone has a serious injury or is hospitalised for a long period: the financial, emotional, and physical impact on the family. Invariably, there is more than one victim in an accident or medical trauma.

How can one earn income or make payments when you are in a coma or severely injured?

If the injured person is the breadwinner, how does his or her family meet their daily living expenses? Not everyone has insurance for this eventuality. And even if they do, there are long time delays and many legal and medical requirements to work through before they receive a benefit payout. If a person, like I did, has to wait over four years before finally receiving compensation from the Road Accident Fund, they would need to be prepared for a long and protracted legal and medical battle.

From a medical and recovery point of view, the patients of

Headway are typically those members of our community who neither have medical aid nor similar benefits, so their medical care and related expenses are absorbed by the NPO. But understandably, the financial support is limited to helping the patient recover from their injuries, not to provide income for their family or to meet their external/personal expenses.

I was one of the lucky ones who had a medical aid and a great job with a great company, yet I also was subjected to a lot of red tape and I felt, to a lesser degree, the medical and financial impact following my accident.

Firstly, while I was in a coma, the medical aid would not take instructions from my brother, claiming he was unauthorised to sign on my behalf. That took a lot of effort to resolve. Secondly, there was the contentious issue of the medical aid refusing to pay certain expenses. My medical bill came to about R1.5 million. The medical-aid company advised that I was personally liable for R300 000. My brother disputed this amount, as all my expenses should have been covered under my medical-aid benefits and hospital plan. The dispute continued until my brother threatened to disclose all this information on various social media sites. Within two days, I received their revised figure and I ended up only paying a meagre R3 000.

If we had not queried, fought and threatened to expose the matter publicly, the medical-aid scheme would have gotten away with a substantial amount of their liability and I would probably still be paying off the debt to this today.

The medical aid was not the only company that required my brother or my family members to have power of attorney to do things on my behalf. Waldek had to jump through hoops to gain access to my bank account in order to pay my bills. To allow him to do this, I managed to scribble my signature on forms I don't recall signing or even seeing.

So many companies are bound by red tape and rules instead of applying some common sense. I appreciate that they need to be prudent to protect both themselves and their clients from fraud. But it is always interesting to see how, when one threatens to expose a company on social media or through other platforms, problems that were once complicated suddenly become very simple.

Another issue that affected me was my job at the bank. I must state that the bank and its personnel were exceptional and provided me with so much support, visited me, and helped in every way possible to alleviate the problems. I received my full salary and special sick-leave benefits for the first three months after the accident in terms of their policy.

Unfortunately, as time went by, I fell into another employee-remuneration policy category. I was now under temporary employment and received 75% of my original salary, with no guarantee of permanent employment. That was like a punch to the solar plexus to me. I was fortunate to be on the positive end of that story. But how many TBI survivors or patients of Headway have no job or other source of income to look forward to?

I managed to receive some compensation from the Road Accident Fund, but that is a long and frustrating story all on its own, steeped in legal wrangles and interpretations of medical reports. It was akin to a chess game wherein my representatives would argue the extent of my injuries and their impact on my life from a physical, mental, spiritual, and emotional point of view; then the state insurer would find their legal and medical representatives to counter every argument and fact my side had presented. The catch in all of this is that it is in the survivor's interest to focus only on the negative aspects, which is completely contrary to endorsing a positive mindset to ensure a speedy and successful recovery.

How the financial side works in practice is that the survivor's lawyers don't get a deposit or upfront fee but are remunerated based on a percentage of the reward or payout from the Road Accident Fund. Owing to the fact that prior to the accident I was a high-potential employee, my attorneys argued that if not for the accident, I would've been promoted as an executive member of the bank within a few years.

But many people, such as labourers or domestic workers, who

have different circumstances in life, have less of a chance of receiving compensation. There is no real incentive for lawyers to take on their cases, and many potential claims fall through the cracks in the compensation system. These survivors either do not claim, or they represent themselves, but without the legal knowledge required, their payouts are, unjustifiably, very small. A great deal of effort is required to convince the Road Accident Fund and their representatives that the survivor is not well enough to go back to work, or to convince the Fund of the survivor's lost opportunities.

I had to listen in to and was subjected to this barrage of questioning and cross-questioning, having to make myself vulnerable and spell out all of my ailments and inadequacies. This had a big impact on my attitude and mental capacity. Every day on my road to recovery, I was trying to be as positive as I could, blocking out the pain and hurts caused by the stigma and rude remarks I was subjected to.

Now, I was having to step back into my past and recount all the negativity, the pain that I was suffering, and the continued effects of the accident on my body and mind. I had to give them reasons as to why I was not 100% fit to work and live my life as before.

I wished, at times, that the people who were making these subjective judgement calls could step into my shoes for a week, or even for a day, and determine exactly the pain, challenges, and emotional torment I was going through. How easy is it to sit on the sidelines and interpret the case in order to make one's findings with no real sense of appreciation or empathy for the other party's challenges?

The thing however that was even more frustrating than this was the fact that I had to lodge a claim against the Road Accident Fund in the first place. I had to do so because the government owns Suikerbosrand Nature Reserve, and thus all roads in the reserve are public ones that are under the control of the road agency and not the management of the reserve. So, in the end, I was forced to sue innocent people who simply fill up their cars with fuel each day; to a degree I was suing myself too. There was absolutely no claim of any sort against, or consequence for, those who managed Suikerbosrand, the guilty party in my eyes. A criminal case was filed against the driver, whose driver's licence was suspended for six months and who was liable for a fine of about R1 000. But the behaviour in the reserve remained the same; they still allow their workers to drive vehicles against the flow of traffic. That's like playing Russian roulette and being shocked and claiming a lack of knowledge of the risks involved after being confronted by the sight of someone's brains splattered on the wall.

I do however have to give the reserve management credit for starting to distribute safety pamphlets two days after my accident. I'm not sure whether the pamphlets were, however, a sign of taking responsibility or of shifting liability. I'm not sure how Adrian and Waldek managed to keep their heads given the situation, but they both had the foresight to take as many photos as possible as evidence for later legal battles. They took as many of these pictures as time and the situation permitted on the day of the accident, but after speaking to a lawyer friend, they decided that additional evidence was required and returned to the reserve to take more. The management of the reserve insisted that my brothers be followed by one of their vehicles ... responsibility or liability? You decide.

Nevertheless, I did receive compensation from the Road Accident Fund. I was fortunate, as so many other people don't have the resources to fight their cause and they lose out completely.

Through my accident and the journey of my recovery, it soon became apparent to me that I have a lot to offer by way of assisting survivors of brain-related injuries and of helping their families to understand what lies ahead for them, both from a medical and a financial point of view.

Headway, I believe, was the best starting point for me. In order to fulfil its mission, the NPO needs sponsorship or financial donations. They are in dire need of funds, so Waldek and I began raising money through our cycling endeavours. We had already competed in the 94.7 Cycle Challenge, which would prove the best opportunity to raise the money. I managed to assemble a team to help Headway that included me, Waldek, Erna, Adrian, my friends, and my work colleagues. This was a lovely and fun-filled way to add value to a very worthy cause.

To me, this has been a personal and purpose-fulfilling means by which to support the patients of Headway and, God willing, I will continue to do more in the future.

41

DOCTORS AREN'T ALWAYS RIGHT

On Friday, 8 June 2018, Erna gave birth to our beautiful daughter, Emilia Wąsowicz, who was born at 3.65 kilograms. Here was another dream being fulfilled, another miracle in my life.

I touched heaven at that moment; I was the happiest dad in the world. And I can assure you that, despite her tiredness and the issues associated with childbirth, Erna was the happiest mom in the world. We were over the moon; we were a complete family. I experienced first-hand, that day, the gift of life.

Immediately, this great event took me back to another miracle in my life. It was now just over eight years since that fateful day in April 2010 when I was knocked off my bicycle by a speeding and negligent driver in Suikerbosrand Nature Reserve. It was eight years since I had cheated death and come out of a coma. And now, by the grace of God and the love and support of my family, I was there to witness the birth of my first child.

I was there to hear my daughter's first cry ... her first sound to announce her arrival into her new world. And, after the doctors and nursing staff had done their bit … little Emilia was wrapped up in a white, teddy-bear patterned Netcare Hospital blanket and placed in my arms. With that symbol came the weight of added responsibility. In addition to protecting and supporting my wife, I now had to care for, empower, teach, support, and protect my baby girl.

Taking Emilia home, as first-time parents, was also an experience. People offer you advice but you have to experience it first-hand to appreciate what you have been told and then work out for yourself what to do.

It was winter in South Africa, so we had to ensure the room was warm enough. We set up the cot in our bedroom and tried to ensure we were as well prepared as we possibly could be. I certainly didn't want Mom and Daughter to become ill. As it turned out, I was the one who got sick. I was diagnosed with swine flu and had to quarantine myself for a few days so as not to infect the rest of my family. These days, I find myself being much worse affected by flu, even if it is normal flu and not anything as severe as swine flu, than I was before the accident. As opposed to experiencing the normal levels of fatigue and body aches associated with flu, I feel such extreme fatigue that I am bed-bound for much longer than other people are, and I feel amplified and throbbing pain in every bone that was broken in the accident.

Those first few weeks at home with Emilia were quite nerve-racking. Erna and I, on edge and inexperienced, listened out for any sound or cry our baby uttered. We weren't used to the hunger cry every two hours on a cold winter's morning. I wasn't prepared for the long winding sessions that followed each feeding, the continual and never-ending diaper changes, and I certainly wasn't prepared for the limited sleep during the night; after which I had to face the responsibilities of my job at the bank the next day. It is however all worth it, and I loved those special moments that presented themselves every day, for instance when my little girl gazed into my eyes, grasped my finger with her tiny hand, fell asleep on my shoulder, or started cooing and smiling for the first time.

We are not the first parents to have endured the newborn stage of a child, and we certainly will not be the last to do so. There are millions of people just like us, with children in varying stages of development. They have made it work, and we will too. There is no manual that comes with parenting. It doesn't matter what religion, culture, family, or country the child is born into; there will be challenges, and every parent will have different ideas. Some tips passed on by friends and family will be useful, and sometimes the new parents will be influenced in how they raise their children by their own upbringing, but the rest of the time, I guess, it's trial and error.

If I think back to how I was raised, I am grateful that my parents always made sure we were safe, educated, and that we went to bed with full stomachs. Family values, traditions, religion, and God were a priority. They sacrificed a great deal for Waldek and me and later for Adrian. The ultimate price was relocating from Communist Poland, leaving their jobs, loved ones, home, and personal belongings, to make a new life for us, the Wąsowicz family, in South Africa. In a way, we were like refugees starting afresh in a new country.

The bottom line is that they did their best and provided a much better life for me and my brothers than what they had endured. I believe each generation wants their children to have a better life or better upbringing than they did. But that is not an easy task in today's age. Divorce, the high number of single parents, peer pressure, technology, malnutrition, and gender-based and child abuse are all factors affecting children and families these days. This has placed added pressure on parents and also children today.

In addition to the birth of Emilia, I have so much to be grateful for over the past ten years. Our second daughter, Isabella, was born on 10 July 2020, right in the middle of the Covid-19 pandemic. We invited Erna's parents to come and visit us and share in this special occasion. However, it proved difficult, given that all local flights were grounded, and that one could only travel between provinces with special permission. This is where the out-of-the-box thinking of Erna's uncle and auntie, Paul and Marteen Michau, who stay fairly close to us, came in handy. Since they would soon be travelling for business purposes to a destination near Nelson Mandela Bay, they offered to give Erna's parents a lift to Johannesburg in their car. Ilse and Otto had to go to the police station to apply for a special pass to travel. They, along with Paul and Marteen, were extra careful not to expose themselves to the virus on their way to Johannesburg. They packed meals so that they didn't have to stop and eat at restaurants. They used the bushes next to the road to make their ablutions. After many hours of travel and a bit of discomfort, they finally got to us. It was wonderful seeing them again, and we were looking forward to the extra help once the little one would arrive.

Two days before the scheduled caesarean birth, we had to undergo a Covid test per the hospital's requirements. While Erna was pregnant, we took all precautions to avoid infection, including social distancing, wearing masks, and continually washing our hands. We even limited our trips to the shops and started ordering most of our groceries online. We also sanitised all products before bringing them into the house. However, we were still a bit nervous about the Covid-19 test, as a positive result would have meant that Erna and Isabella would've been moved into a ward full of Covid-19 patients after the delivery, potentially increasing Isabella's chances of infection. Also, I wouldn't have been allowed in to support Erna during the birth.

Our vigilance and prayers paid off, as our tests came back negative, and on the morning of Friday, 10 July, we made our way to the hospital. We had packed a hospital bag for Erna and the baby; however, I hadn't packed one for myself, as we were informed that, owing to Covid-19, fathers could no longer stay in the hospital overnight. The father was only allowed to stay for three hours after the birth, bonding with the newborn and providing support to his partner.

I personally saw this as an opportunity to go back home and celebrate with all of my family and friends over video chats. My dream of smashing a couple of drinks was cut short when we were told that the rules had been relaxed and that fathers were now allowed to stay longer after the birth so long as they stayed in the hospital for the duration of their visit. As the saying goes, "If you leave, you leave for good". So, there I was, for the next three days, without a change of clothes. Luckily, the hospital allowed for friends or family to drop off bags at the entrance; the staff would bring the stuff to the ward. This is once again where Paulo came in. Not only did he bring me another shirt or two and another pair of socks (which I was now so fond of putting on my feet), but he also, bless his generous heart, brought me a bottle of single-malt Scottish whisky. I could now see my second princess being born, be by my wife's side, and still have video-chat parties with our loved ones!

The birth went well, with Isabella being born at a healthy weight of 3.6 kilograms. She swallowed a bit of amniotic fluid and was placed in the neonatal section for observation, but recovered quickly and was returned to our arms within an hour.

We came home on Sunday and were overjoyed by Emilia's happiness in meeting her little sister. Things were perfect … until the next day, when Ilse developed a mild fever and a slightly sore throat. By Tuesday, her symptoms had worsened, and we really started to worry. I took her to the nearest drive-through testing station, and we were told that we'd have the results in 24 hours.

Otto and I both developed fevers on Tuesday as well. Erna insisted we get tested, but I was a bit stubborn, and we didn't go on that day. We did, however, start taking precautions. We made sure that Erna, together with the kids, was isolating in one side of the house. We also sent our domestic worker and our gardener home in order not to expose them to the virus. So, I was the cook, the house cleaner, the dishwasher, the laundry man, and the gardener from then onwards.

On Wednesday, Otto and I went for a test. Later that day, Ilse received her results. She had tested positive for Covid. She went into isolation in a room. Otto and I brought her food, drinks, and medicine throughout the day, being careful to avoid close contact. On Thursday, Otto and I learnt that we too were positive. Erna didn't wait and packed the kids into the car and drove to the testing station. The next day, their test results came back positive too. Although everyone in the household had Covid, our doctors advised us to self-isolate from each other as much as possible, to wear masks, and to keep sanitising surfaces in a bid to try and keep our respective viral loads as low as possible.

Otto and I battled for a couple of days with fatigue, sore throats, and a fever that kept spiking and retreating. Ilse also suffered from fatigue and fever, and her chest symptoms, a persistent dry cough and shortness of breath, progressively worsened. Otto completely lost his sense of taste and of smell. Luckily, Erna and the kids appeared to be largely asymptomatic.

The worst part of this experience was the unknown. Every time Isabella, only a week old, would sneeze or make a little wheezing noise, we feared the worst, but we couldn't take her to the paediatrician or even to a GP for a check-up, as we all had to self-isolate at home. We sent recordings of Isabella's breathing to her paediatrician and had a consultation via Skype, but were not 100% reassured that she was okay, given the lack of a physical examination. But thankfully, in the end, the kids, Erna, Otto, and I were unscathed.

Ilse's cough, shortness of breath, and oxygen-saturation levels were however worsening day by day. Within a week, her chest had closed so much that she struggled to breathe, and she was admitted via the emergency room to the Netcare Waterfall City Hospital. Her X-rays showed that she had developed Covid-pneumonia, a very serious condition that necessitated her spending ten days in a high-care ward. We weren't even allowed to go and visit her. Luckily, my cycling friend David Goncalves is a psychologist who works at Netcare Waterfall City Hospital and was able to visit Ilse and give her great support by speaking to her like an individual and not just another Covid patient.

Meanwhile, Erna and I were under immense pressure. With very little sleep, and with doubt and worry in our hearts, we had to take care of a newborn, a very busy toddler, and Erna's bedridden dad (before he recovered) while I was also ill and Erna was still recovering from the caesarean operation. I did my best to stay level-headed, but there were scary times. I recall lying in bed a little bit longer one morning, as I wanted to recover, feeling completely drained, and strangely empty. I felt myself slipping slowly into an abyss of depression. Thankfully, I didn't allow myself to dwell on this for too long. I got up and started doing my normal daily household chores and parenting, and all of a sudden, I started feeling a little better. Being productive and helping the rest of my family members was actually helping me.

As was the case following my bike accident in 2010, our family received prayers and immense support from friends and other relatives during the crisis. We all managed to get through it, and Erna and I could start enjoying our growing family.

My two little girls have brought immense joy and happiness into my life. I cannot help but think how much I would've missed those little, special moments. Like when Emilia wants me to lie down on the floor next to her with my eyes closed, pretending to sleep, while she covers me with a blanket, gives me her favourite sleep toy, and pretends to read me a bedtime story. Such times allow me to find peace in the moment, an art which sometimes slips away from all of us once we become adults. Or when Isabella is distressed until her eyes meet mine and I hold her in my arms and all of her worries disappear like shadows dissolved by the sunshine of her huge smile.

If I'd given up all those years ago, this wouldn't be a reality. Back in 2010, according to the doctors at Union Hospital, I had a less-than 5% chance of survival, and if I was lucky enough to make it, I would likely be in an incapacitated state, paralysed and confined to a wheelchair.

Doctors are not always right and miracles can happen. In my personal opinion, doctors' views are based on averages and historical knowledge; no one has ever understood the entire universe, and no one ever will; so with utter determination and focus, one can rise above the statistics – you can rise above what we know and understand today.

42

MY PARTING MESSAGE

The journeys of recovery after the accident, of self-discovery, and of newfound purpose, have not been easy. Their catalyst was being knocked off my bicycle, spending 14 days in a coma, and then having to find the inner strength and will to fight for and regain control of my life.

My life is different now. My back still hurts. My knee pains. During winter, and despite wearing long pyjamas, I pull a ski sock, whose foot I have cut off, over my knee to keep it warm and the pain at bay. My shoulder still hurts every day, and there is nothing I can do about it. I did ask Dr Michael Laric to remove the titanium pole and plates from it, but he was unable to do so given the high level of calcification that occurred. My teeth and jaw still hurt. Sometimes when I walk it feels like someone is taking a chisel and hammering it into the roots of my teeth. I am still freaked out by the magnification of light in my right eye and the flash I see every time I hear a clicking sound when I'm falling asleep. I get very fatigued, struggle with concentrating for long periods of time, and am sometimes acutely aware of my short-term memory lapses.

Deep inside, although I do try to hide it from myself, I am afraid of what is to come. Will I require a back operation in a couple of years? Will I be in a wheelchair again? Will my shoulder give way, and will I be left with a dead arm? Will I develop epilepsy? Will Alzheimer's or dementia set in? Will I be trapped in my body and mind again?

These are my fears. However, what I do hold close to my heart is the understanding that you must be happy with every new wrinkle on your face, every grey hair, and each and every hair that falls out. Be happy to grow older. It is a blessing; the alternative is not youth but the cold and hard ground.

The message I have tried to convey throughout this book is simple: I was not a perfect man before the accident; I was not a lucky man in my accident; I am not a special man since my accident; but I am a man who believed in his own identity, who refused to give up, who remained positive and managed to keep his eye on the end goal.

I had to reach deep inside and take control of my life and my destiny. I decided not to allow one man's stupidity to ruin my life and the things that I love about it, including cycling. I am now a married man, sharing my life with an incredible woman, Erna, and our beautiful daughters, Emilia and Isabella. I am excited about what the future holds in store for me.

You can read my story and make excuses for yourself by saying any of the following:

- "My circumstances are different to yours."
- "I am older than you."
- "My injury was different to yours."
- "I do not have the same support you did."

You could carry on indefinitely: "I do not…I do not…I do not…".

There are others out there who, injured far worse than I was, have also recovered. On the other side, some who were hurt far less severely than I was, have not overcome their injuries. There are many factors that contributed to my recovery from such a debilitating situation.

To conclude my story, I wish to leave you with a summary of some of the major factors and concepts that worked for me. I hope these will be of benefit to you and help you with your life's journey, no matter your circumstances.

Firstly, give thanks to your Creator. I survived and now am alive by the grace of God. It was a miracle. I do believe in miracles and the power of prayer. Humanity does not know everything. We thought Newton understood the universe until Einstein came along. Now we understand the universe through Einstein's theories but will only do so until someone else comes along.

Secondly, and following on very closely from the above, feed off the encouragement and energy of others, especially your loved ones. It was the support, care, and unending love of my family and close friends, acquaintances, and of course the help of the doctors and the nursing staff, that helped me enormously.

Thirdly, it is important to have something to aim for and desire in life, but it is even more important to take action by breaking down those massive, ultimate end goals into smaller, achievable ones. Otherwise, your ultimate goal will remain merely a wish. It was my burning desire to survive and cycle again that helped me to recover.

Fourthly, develop a mental attitude that will help you overcome the pain barrier and continue through your rehab process, becoming stronger and stronger every day. One's mindset and attitude are the most important drivers a person can have. I made a decision to overcome the pain I was experiencing and to no longer live life as a complainer or as a victim of pain. I don't talk about or dwell on my pain any more.

Fifthly, it helps to have a role model. My grandfather, my superhero and role model, was another sense of encouragement and focus on my road to recovery.

I also took heart from the dream I had just after emerging from my coma; the one in which I fought and defeated a lion.

This told me that I was in control of my destiny, my recovery, my life. I needed to act and to act decisively. I had to push aside those demons in my head and the pain I was going through and concentrate on living, one day at a time.

I do not believe that my accident happened for a reason. I do believe, however, that I survived for a reason. Since the accident, I have discovered a part of myself that wasn't there before; to be a person who reaches out to offer insight and help to others.

My road to recovery has highlighted a number of viewpoints that I hold very dear in my life. These are my core values and beliefs. Many of these I have shared throughout my book. For my parting message, I have summarised a few of my personal philosophies in the hope that one or two will resonate with you, and that you can apply them in your own life.

- **Every day is an opportunity, do not waste it.**
- **You are not the centre of the universe, so don't concentrate on yourself.**
- **Make a conscious decision that you will recover.**
- **Find a person who has suffered more than you have, and let him or her be your inspiration.**
- **Find hope in little things that you can keep close to yourself and turn to when most needed.**
- **Social stigma is not based on facts but rather on the opinions of others.**
- **Doctors are not always right, and miracles can happen.** Doctors' views are based on averages and theoretical knowledge; you can rise above the statistics. Remember, one of the smartest people within our lifetime, Stephen Hawking, was a man who could not move or speak, but the whole world rose up and listened to him.
- **Remember that you were never perfect to begin with.**
- **Choose your identity and strive towards that in every instance.** If you want to be the person that you

were before trauma, choose to be that person and try in everything you do to be him or her. By choosing not to be that because your doctors, your family, or your friends say that you cannot, you will be fulfilling that destiny. By choosing to get better, you at least have a chance, regardless of how small it may be, of it coming to fruition.

- **If you are still alive, irrespective of your current situation, smile.** Things could always be worse.
- **There is always a plan B in life.** There may be times when things are not under your control; play the hand that you are dealt.
- **The pendulum has two sides.** Being caught in the rain while walking home sucks, but being stuck in a hospital bed without the ability to feel the rain on your face is heartbreaking.

Perhaps you are one of those people reading this book who is suffering from some trauma, other affliction, or dread disease. Perhaps you are facing something different, some form of adversity in your life.

You have to be strong mentally to rise above this. Your attitude, your life philosophies, and your inner strength need to be aligned and focused, unwavering and strong, not only for today, but for every day.

My message to you is do not give up and do not quit. The storms of life will eventually pass. Only you can control your mindset during the journey of recovery. Miracles do happen daily, even in this day and age.

PICTURES

Waldek (left), aged three, and me, aged two.

Feeling sad ... as play time was over. Notice the knees.

Waldek and I twinning in style (thanks, Mom).

Our Holy Communion: me with Waldek, Mom, and Dad in front of the Roman Catholic Church in Wojkowice Kościelne.

My grandfather, Zenon Muraszewski (the *Sołtys*), on the steps of the Palace of Culture and Science in Warsaw.

Our house in Poland that was divided into three apartments. We lived in the apartment on the top floor.

The Suikerbosrand Nature Reserve service vehicle that smashed into me.

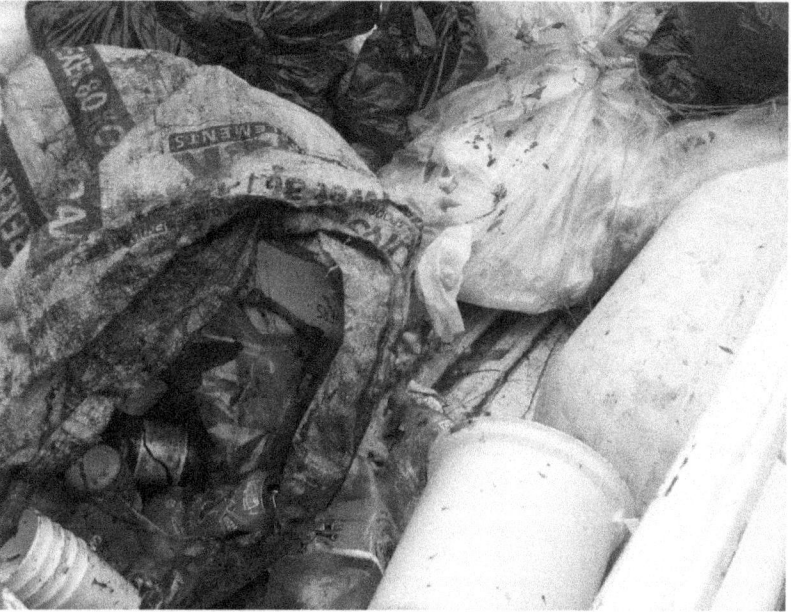

Soft landing at the back of the service vehicle.

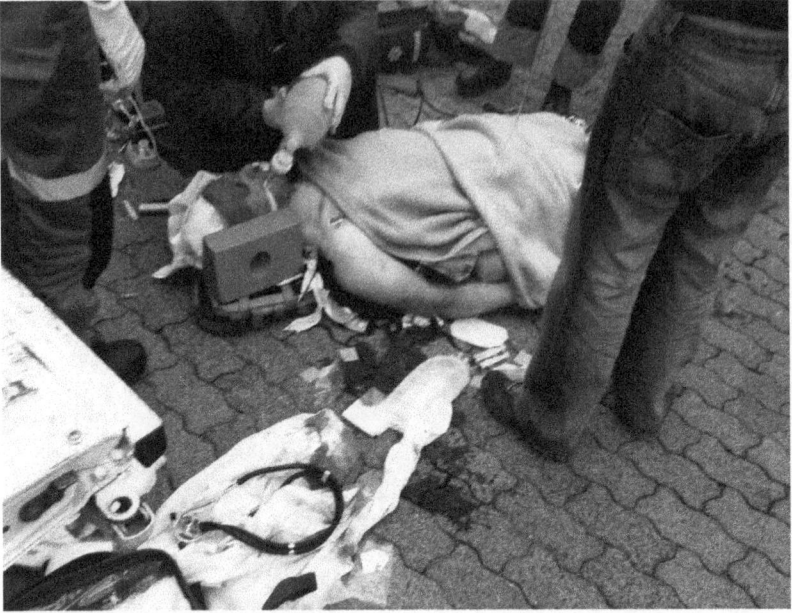
On the scene, being stabilised by the paramedics.

My shredded pride and joy.

My bloody helmet.

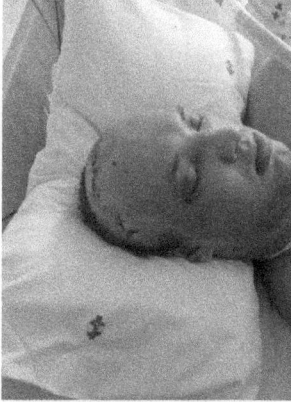

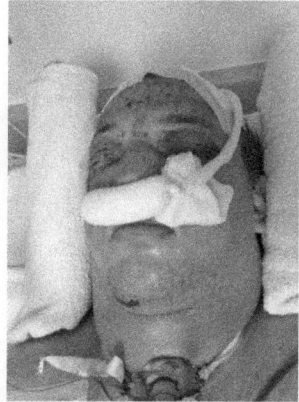

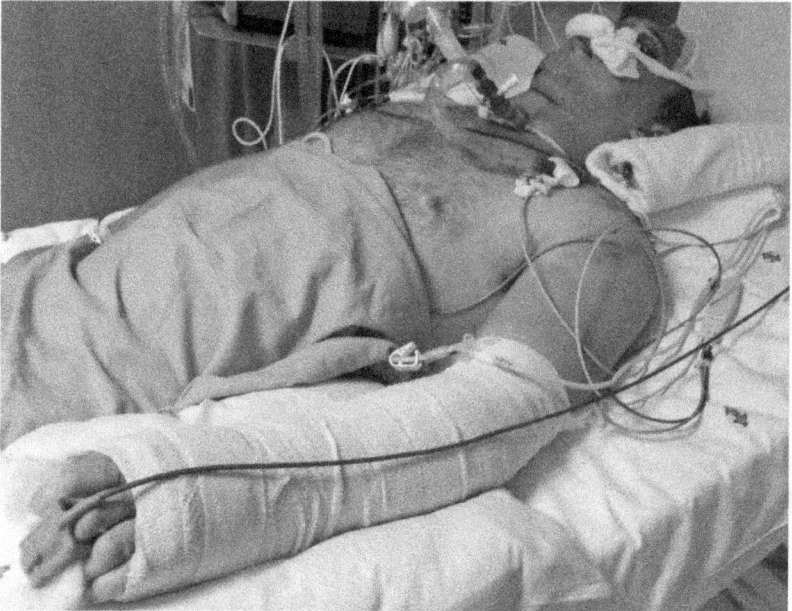

Photos of me in hospital, taken about three to five weeks after the accident.

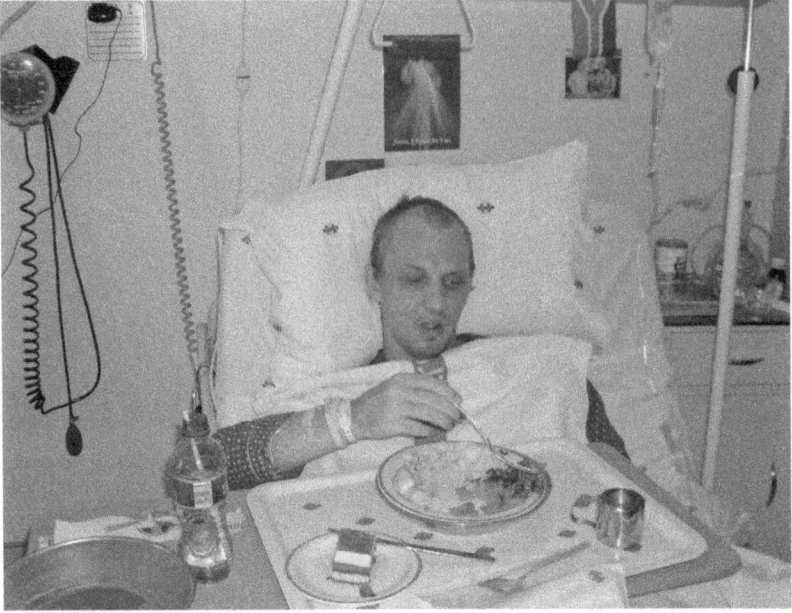
In hospital with the pictures my mom stuck on the walls to humanise me.

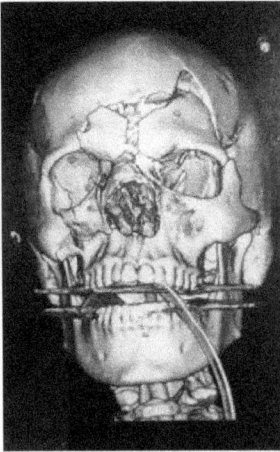
Face of the broken man.

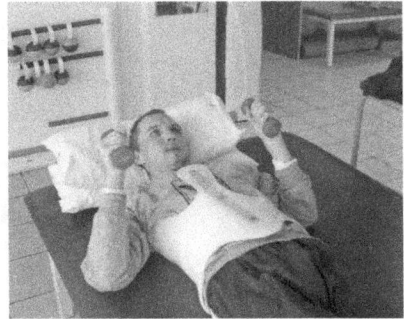
Doing my recovery exercises in mid-July ... with my Lance Armstrong "Livestrong" wristband on.

World-class Cervélo R3 ... one of my sources of inspiration.

My first ride after the accident. Man/cyclist logic: I didn't want to risk my new Cervélo R3 getting damaged, so I used my old mountain bike.

Riding with Adrian ... and we are still riding together.

Getting ready to ride with Waldek and Adrian in preparation for the 94.7 Cycle Challenge.

Riding the Cape Epic and feeling magic … while dying inside from exhaustion. (Picture © sportograf.com)

Brothers: wet, muddy, and pushing on. (Picture © sportograf.com)

Finally at the finish of The Epic. What a feeling! (Picture © sportograf.com)

On top of Col de L'Iseran, in France, a Tour de France climb.

Climbing high on France tour with Waldek.

Breathtaking views in France.

With Erna in Poland after my family gave her roses.

Listening to a violinist playing for us, just before the dancing started.

My groomsmen (from left to right): Paulo, Waldek, Heinrich, Adrian, and Sacha.

Erna and I with the beautiful Carmen (left), Ava – the cutest baby – on my lap, and Alexander (also known to everyone as "Sacha").

The two of us on our special day.

Erna and I with our parents.

Emilia and Daddy.

Princess Emilia (as she is known at her crèche).

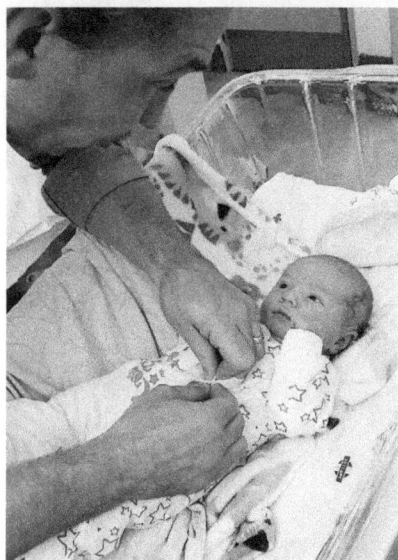

Daddy dressing Isabella up in hospital after her birth.

Isabella chilling with Daddy.

My love for cycling seems to have passed to the next generation! I'm sure Isabella will soon join her sister on a bicycle and that it will strengthen their relationship as it did for Adrian, Waldek, and me.